D0168882

The Power of Love for Teens

True Stories Written by Teens
From the Pages of **Guideposts**.

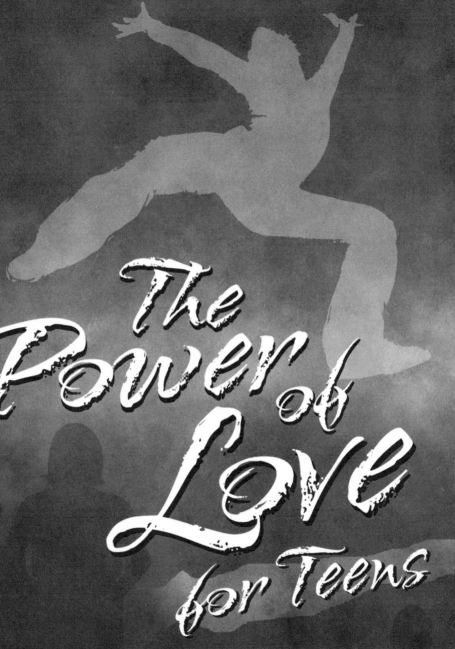

The Power of Love for Teens

True Stories Written by Teens
From the Pages of **Guideposts**

Ideals Publications • Nashville, Tennessee

ISBN 0-8249-4629-4

Published by Ideals Publications
A division of Guideposts
535 Metroplex Drive, Suite 250
Nashville, Tennessee 37211
www.idealsbooks.com

Printed and bound in the U.S.A.

Library of Congress CIP data on file

10 9 8 7 6 5 4 3 2 1

Contents

The Power of Love for Family 6

The Power of Love at School 42

The Power of Love for Friends 72

The Power of Love in Action.......................108

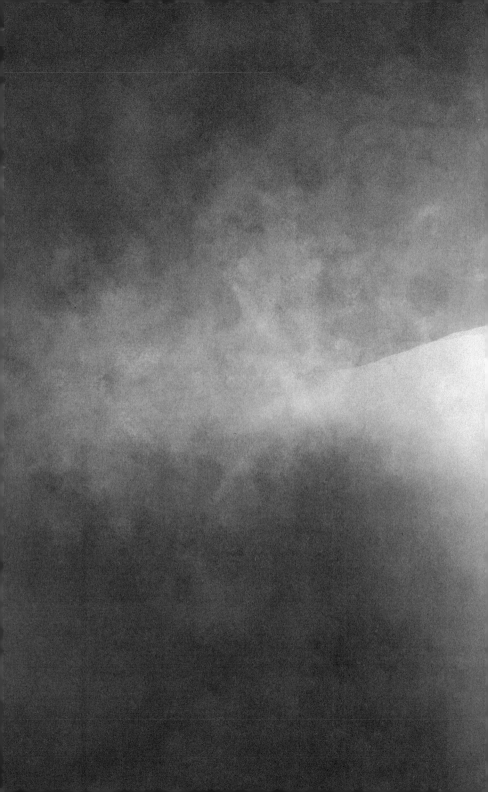

Turkey Day Takeover

KAREN LANGLEY

*M*om did it again. I was used to her inviting people to our house for Thanksgiving. But *twenty-four* people? I couldn't even find enough forks to set the table!

Our first guests had arrived earlier that morning—three guys from Navy boot camp. The original plan was to host one recruit. Mom came back from the Navy base with three.

It's not that I mind a full house. I have great memories of Thanksgivings from when I was a kid—dozens of cousins running around, aunts tripping over each other in the kitchen, uncles watching football. That's how Thanksgiving is *supposed* to be—lots of relatives and a big, traditional dinner.

But ever since my family moved across the country, away from our relatives, Mom has filled our house with a random assortment of guests. Foreign exchange students. Newly divorced women. Oddballs she met at the grocery store. You name it.

I wandered into the living

That best portion of a good man's life are his little, nameless, unremembered acts of kindness and of love.

WILLIAM WORDSWORTH

room, where my grandfather was setting up chairs at a borrowed folding table. "Need some help, Pop Pop?"

"Oh, thanks, sweetie," he said. "I think your mother's invited the whole town!"

I sighed. When I'd heard that Pop Pop and Grandmom would be visiting us for Thanksgiving this year, I'd figured Mom would nix the stray people invites. It seemed kind of rude to subject my grandparents to a houseful of random people they didn't know. *I barely knew most of the people Mom had invited!*

There is only one happiness in life: to love and be loved.

GEORGE SAND

The doorbell rang, and the next installment of guests burst in. Mr. and Mrs. Kerney, a couple from town, tramped in with their six young kids. Right on their heels came Mom's friend, Mrs. Moberg, and her two sons. Soon there were people everywhere.

At dinner, my turkey name card placed me at the end of the dining room table, between Mrs. Moberg and a fussy Kerney baby. *How'd I get so lucky?* I wondered, as a pudgy fist smacked my shoulder.

Pop Pop and Grandmom sat at the other end of the table, near one of the recruits. They chatted the entire meal about military stuff. *Glad I'm getting all this quality time with my grandparents.*

After dinner, Mom suggested that while

everyone was together in one room, we each share something we're thankful for—an annual tradition at our house.

Mrs. Kerney spoke up. "I'm so grateful to this wonderful family for opening up *I live and* their home to us." Then she thanked *love in God's* God for a bunch of stuff, and her *peculiar light.* eyes got watery. I'd forgotten till now MICHELANGELO that the Kerney family had seven kids until a week ago. Their baby girl had died, after months in and out of the hospital.

Would I be grateful to God if someone in my family had just died?

Mrs. Moberg thanked my family for sharing our day with her and her sons. I remembered the shock we all had a few months ago when Mrs. Moberg's husband left her and the kids. He'd seemed like such a nice guy. Now they were in the middle of a nasty divorce.

I guess this is probably their first holiday without their dad around.

One of the Navy guys said how much it meant to them to be able to be with a family on Thanksgiving.

All of a sudden it was my turn.

"I'm thankful for a full house—that all of you could share this day with us."

Whoa . . . What did I just say?

I looked around the room at our guests. Pop Pop sat by one of the recruits. He sure seemed to enjoy having someone to swap military stories with. The youngest Kerney girl fiddled with her pigtails. The

'Tis the most tender part of love, each other to forgive.

JOHN SHEFFIELD

Navy guys and my family are white; Mom's friend and her two sons are Filipino; the Kerneys are black.

We sure make a funny-looking family.

Then it hit me. I'd been wrong about the meaning of Thanksgiving. Sure, it's great to be with relatives. And it's great to say thanks for my blessings. But what's the point in *saying* I'm thankful if I'm not willing to *share* my blessings—including my grandparents and the rest of my family?

The day turned out to be one of the best Thanksgivings ever. I held the Kerney baby, who stopped fussing once he got some food in his belly. My brother and one of the Moberg boys wore crazy wigs and performed Weird Al songs. The Navy guys told stories about life in boot camp, which gave me something else to be thankful for—that *I'm* not in boot camp. Later in the afternoon, a bunch of us headed outside to play football. It wouldn't be right not to play football on Thanksgiving. And everything about this day was *just right.*

Mom's Old Kentucky Home

WHITNEY WEITZEL

My mother danced around the kitchen in her long, cotton dress, lifting the lid off the pot on the stove to stir the contents. Occasionally she came to the dinner table to ask if I had washed my hands before devouring my slices of orange. I looked up, juice on my face, and said, "Mom, they're clean!" Then I held my hands up as proof, not realizing that the grime under my fingernails and in the creases of my knuckles was too dark to be missed. It was during this time every day that we discussed what was going on in our lives, analyzing things from my six-year-old point of view.

> *I have loved you with an everlasting love.*
> JEREMIAH 31:3

From time to time these talks led to my mother's description of her childhood in Anchorage, a small town outside Louisville, Kentucky. She told me of a place where she could skip across the street to her best friend's house, where they spoke in rich southern accents about horse shows and about Tommy Austin, who once set off a firecracker in his hand. In the summertime she could run to the end of town and across a meadow to the country club, where she swam for hour upon hour.

There was a dime store up the block, and her mother sent her there on errands. On Sundays everyone gathered in Saint Luke's Episcopal Church and worshiped together. Afterward, they returned to their houses for potluck brunches with cheese grits and mint juleps. There was only one school in town, and the parents of the students had taken the same courses as their children.

My mother made it sound like a magical place, where nothing ever went wrong and everyone always smiled. But when I finally flew to Louisville, I did not like the area. It was late June, I was much older, and I wasn't prepared for the humidity that enveloped me as I stepped from the airport.

We are all pencils in the hand of a writing God who is sending love letters to the world.

MOTHER TERESA

I was with my mother, visiting for the week of my cousin's wedding. We loaded up and then climbed into our rented car. My mother adjusted the air conditioner, then we left the airport and found ourselves downtown. There were shopping complexes and gas stations everywhere, and a yellow haze had settled between the buildings. I began to wonder if the sunny, grassy Eden my mother had told me about was all in her imagination. As we drove on, the mini-malls thinned out, and the roads slimmed to two lanes. Maple trees lined the streets, and I began to see the beauty of the South.

There is never much trouble in any family where the children hope someday to resemble their parents.

WILLIAM LYON PHELPS

Before long we came to Anchorage. It was just as I had pictured—rolling pastures where horses grazed and gardens rich with vegetables that would soon be ripe. The houses had windows with lace curtains, front doors with brass knobs, and white stone gates.

My mother slowed the car as we passed the drugstore where she had her first job and the grocery store where she used to buy sugarcane for five cents. As we turned down the streets, we passed the places where she had tasted life for the first time. Watching her face, I could see all the memories flood back. For each house there was a story. We drove by the first house she had lived in, and she told me about the secret panel inside that concealed a space that had been used to hide escaped slaves.

We drove on, past the stables where she had boarded her horses and past her best friend's house.

She took me to the country club and to the creek where she had spent hours catching tadpoles with her brother.

We headed down one more street. The houses were smaller and closer together. As she swung the car into one of the driveways, she said, "And this is Saint Luke's." I recalled that it was one of her favorite places to be. She looked forward to Sundays because the whole town assembled together in one tiny room. They forgot their petty arguments and came in their best clothes to be among the people who made up their lives.

We parked in the empty lot, got out, and headed for the door to the chapel. It was locked, so I followed her around to the back. A light step had entered her stride, and her arms swung loosely at her sides. This was where she was comfortable. The back door happened to be open, and she smiled as we stepped inside. A quiet sigh escaped her as she looked around. "This is the choir room," she said. "Sunday school was down there." She pointed to a flight of stairs and a hallway with finger paintings taped to the walls.

She looked the other way, at another flight of

Love is not love which alters when it alteration finds or bends with the remover to remove.

WILLIAM SHAKESPEARE

stairs. She moved to them and began slowly ascending. "I can remember walking up these stairs in my choir robe every Sunday after I turned twelve." She lightly touched the handrail as she took each step. I walked behind her without a word, listening because she wanted to tell someone, but quiet because this was her time. She knew I was there, and yet she didn't. She had gone back in her mind and was twelve again, wearing her choir robe.

Though I speak with the tongues of men and of angels and have not love, I am become as sounding brass or tinkling cymbal.

1 CORINTHIANS 13:1

As we came to the top of the stairs, there was a door propped open. She paused before she went in, preparing herself for what she might see. The two of us stepped inside the chapel and stood a minute, taking in the beauty of the stained glass windows surrounded by walls of stone. The pews were a rich, dark brown, and the colored light from the windows fell on the glossy wood.

She began to walk down the aisle toward the altar, seeing the people she grew up with as she went. She came to the choir pews and sat down in the first row. "This was where I sat. For a long time I was the smallest one in the choir, until I was about fifteen or sixteen. They still treated me like I was the smallest one, though." She stood again and turned slowly, as if dancing to music that swept through her, drinking everything in. "There are so many memories here. . . . This must be the place that reminds me most of my childhood."

It was then I realized what I was seeing. This was a piece of my mother. A piece that, with the passing years, I had heard less and less

Love conquers all things; let us, too, surrender to love.

VIRGIL

of. Maybe it was because she no longer talked about it, but I knew more likely it was because I was no longer there to listen. I was growing up and busy figuring out my life and never paused to hear about hers. She was always listening to me. There was really so little I knew about her.

It was in Saint Luke's that I saw the little girl in my mother, and surprisingly, I saw myself. I had places like this that were very dear to me, and I wondered if someday I too would be dancing in the very place where I learned what living was about.

On a Rainy Summer Day

KATHERINE CRISALLI

I didn't know my grandfather well. He'd had Alzheimer's for more than ten years—almost as long as I could remember—so whoever he really was got lost somewhere inside the vacant haze of the illness. Most of what I knew about him came from stories I'd heard my mom tell. Once a year, when I went with my family to Missouri to visit my mom's relatives, there would be that painful day or two we'd spend with him in the nursing home. I used to stare at him sitting hunched and frail on a hard chair, thinking that if I looked at him long enough, I'd eventually catch a glimpse of the gentle, funny, hardworking man that my mother always talked about.

> *There is only one happiness in life: to love and be loved.*
>
> GEORGE SAND

Virtually the only thing I knew about him in relation to me was that, when I was little, he used to have tea parties with me. My grandma had a set of plastic dishes that I'd fill with water, pretending I was brewing an exotic elixir. My mom always said that he'd sit with me for hours on end, long after everyone else in the family had found other things that they needed to do, sipping warm water and listening to my chatter. She said he made me laugh.

I didn't want to believe what everyone said— that his disease was irreversible. At our church every Sunday, the congregation is told to pray "for those intentions we hold in the silence of our hearts." I used to pray that I could be nicer to my sister, and that a sudden plague would kill all of the world's broccoli, and then I'd tag on, "And please make Papa get better, God." I was childishly confident that all of these requests would be met promptly; after all, if God were omnipotent, then it stood to reason that he would be efficient too. Of course, it didn't happen like that.

> *For love is heaven and heaven is love.*
> SIR WALTER SCOTT

My grandfather passed away on July 19, the summer before last. We were, like most families who have faced the death of a loved one after a long illness, caught somewhere between grief and thankfulness that he wouldn't have to suffer anymore. His funeral was a few days later in Sarcoxie, the tiny town in the southwest corner of Missouri where he built my grandmother's house with his own two hands and made a living for his family by the sweat of his brow.

I stood in the graveyard that day, looking at the casket through misty eyes while a slow, summer drizzle fell on the gravestones. Maybe the weather made the ordeal easier to handle; it seemed like the world was crying gentle tears along with those of us standing around the fresh grave. As they lowered my grandfather's casket into the ground, all I could think was, "This was the man who had tea parties with me." It seemed so desperately sad to me that that was all I really knew of him.

How do I love thee? Let me count the ways. I love thee to the depth and breadth and height my soul can reach when feeling out of sight for the ends of Being and ideal Grace.

ELIZABETH BARRETT BROWNING

We went back to my grandma's house in silence. Usually when our family comes to Sarcoxie in the summer we have a family reunion, a day of potluck lunches and "do-you-remember" stories, when the grown-ups relax in aluminum chairs on the lawn and the kids and teenagers dart around them in bathing suits, playing a game that is tag and sardines and a water fight all in one. That year, the family reunion wasn't the festive occasion of summers past. Lunch was a quiet affair, and afterward there was silence as people read or napped or sat sunk in their own reflections. Outside, the rain grew from a gentle shower to hard bullet-like drops, accompanied by distant flashes of lightning.

It was mid-afternoon when we heard a cry from my grandmother in the kitchen. Thinking something was wrong, everyone rushed in. She was standing transfixed at the window over the sink. I squeezed in beside her and pushed back the red chiffon curtains. The sight before me was amazing.

Ah, love, let us be true to one another!

MATTHEW ARNOLD

A shallow, grassy ditch meanders along the side of her house, ending where it runs into the road. Once there was a garden behind the house and the ditch was for drainage; but the garden had long since gone to seed, and the ditch had been dry for many years. That day, there had been so much rain that a waist-deep river was running in the yard. The oldest people in the room hadn't seen that much water there since they were children.

There was a loud crack as the stubborn screen door at the back of the house opened and snapped closed. I got just a glimpse of two, small bodies in bathing suits—my sister Andrea and my cousin Pete—before hearing two, high Tarzan yells and a pair of splashes. I looked back out the window and, sure enough, there were Andrea and Pete dog-paddling down the ditch in the warm rain, shriek-ing with laughter.

Everyone else was outside in moments. Some of the teenagers made a raft to float down our river—first a Styrofoam one, which collapsed, dunking its passengers, and then an old inflatable kiddie pool, which overturned midway through one of the rapids and then clung like plastic wrap while everyone tried to extricate themselves. The adults stood in the driveway, barefoot and clutching umbrellas, calling out suggestions when they weren't doubled over laughing.

The mind has a thousand eyes, and the heart but one; yet the light of a whole life dies when love is done.

FRANCIS WILLIAM BOURDILLON

It was a wonderful day. The old aluminum lawn chairs came out after all, and the grown-ups sat around telling "do-you-remember" stories, while the young fry raced back and forth playing a game that was tag and sardines and a ready-made water fight all in one. As for me, I wound up wading in the shallow water along the edge of the ditch with my jeans rolled up, letting the cool water and tiny weeds caress my feet. I was thinking about some-thing I had read earlier that day on one of my grandfather's funeral cards: "The Lord is my shepherd, I shall not want. He maketh me to lie down in green pastures; he leadeth me beside the still waters; he restoreth my soul."

At that moment, I did not want. I was there amid the emerald green of the Missouri landscape, beside my own personal river, which had restored my soul and the souls of my family. I would never look at tragedy the same way again, because I had suddenly been shown that there is always brightness waiting just around the corner. I knew beyond a doubt that my grandfather was somewhere close and that he was smiling. And if that isn't a miracle, then I don't know what is.

Love looks not with the eyes but with the mind, and therefore is wing'd Cupid painted blind.

WILLIAM SHAKESPEARE

Trusting Tom

THIRZA PEEVEY

I never felt comfortable around men. I didn't trust them. My father was distant and barely made time for me. I didn't have any brothers or even a male teacher I looked up to. I shied away from the boys in grade school. They teased me about my weight. In high school, I'd escape to the library and sit on the floor in the second-to-last row. That's where my favorite shelf was—the horse books. By sopho-more year I'd made my way through most of them—*Come on Seabiscuit!*; *My Horses, My Teachers*; *Grooming to Win*. One day I came across *The Will to Win* by Jane McIlvaine. I'd lost myself in the world of steeplechase, a popular sport in England, where strong horses ran three-mile courses dotted with high fences and hedges. Anxiously I followed the story of an underdog named Jay Trump as he raced his way to unexpected victory. "I wish I had his courage," I thought as I closed the book.

It's Love that makes the world go round!

W. S. GILBERT

After graduation I left my parents' Kentucky farm for a career in horse grooming. The first job I landed was in Maryland. There, in the stable manager's office, I noticed a photo of a familiar horse. It was Jay Trump. The stable manager's brother had broken him in. My next job was at a hunt club in Maryland. Again, Jay Trump came into my life. He had trained at the club. Looking at his photographs, I wondered why he kept popping up. "It's probably just coincidence," I thought. "But what if God has a message for me in that horse?"

One message I got loud and clear was, horse grooming doesn't pay the bills. I had to move back to Kentucky, back to my parents' house. I unpacked my things and put away the high school yearbook still sitting on my shelf. All my former classmates were married with families; some had successful careers. I was alone, working for $5.25 an hour. In the relationship department, I was more of an underdog than Jay Trump. No amount of courage would ever change that. I only hoped I had a shot at the grooming job I was interviewing for in the morning.

Many waters cannot quench love, neither can the floods drown it.

SONG OF SOLOMON 8:7

When I got to Pin Oak Farm, a man drove up in a truck. His skin was ruddy and his build was slight. "You must be Thirza," he said with a British accent. "I'm Tom, the stable manager. Let's get started."

He escorted me around the grounds. I avoided making eye contact. "Will I be this way with every man I ever meet?" I wondered.

Tom turned to me. "If you want the job, it's yours." I looked at my feet and nodded.

I steered clear of Tom until he called me over one day. "The colt Peaks and Valleys hurt his leg," Tom said. "I'll need you to help change the bandages."

I went to Peaks and Valleys' stall. "It's okay, boy, we're going to fix you right up," I said, rubbing his back.

"You're good with him." I turned and saw Tom behind me. "Really, you've got the touch. Not everyone can keep an injured colt calm." He set down an armload of bandages, cotton, and antibiotics. Tom stroked the colt's leg. Gently, he cut off the old bandages. Peaks and Valleys didn't move a muscle.

> *Doubt thou the stars are fire;*
> *doubt that the sun doth move;*
> *Doubt truth to be a liar; But never doubt I love.*
>
> WILLIAM SHAKESPEARE

"I've never seen anyone do that without the colt kicking," I said.

"I guess I've got the touch too," Tom said, then winked at me.

My face got hot. Still, I couldn't help but smile before I looked away.

Tom and I got to work. I handed the bandages

to him to wrap Peaks and Valleys' leg. We talked to the colt to calm him. And we talked to each other. We talked about horses—the best equipment, riders we liked, horses we followed. I could hardly believe I was hearing the sound of my own voice. This wasn't so hard. "Something about this guy makes me feel comfortable. He's so kind. He treats me with real respect."

"One of my favorite horses I read about in a book a long time ago—this horse called Jay Trump."

"The steeplechase champ! I know him well. My uncle trained him," Tom said. "Funny, almost no one I've met in the States knows about steeplechase." We wrapped Peaks and Valleys' leg and talked about races Jay Trump had won.

But true love is a durable fire, In the mind ever burning, Never sick, never old, never dead, From itself never turning.

SIR WALTER RALEIGH

The next morning the staff took the horses out for exercise. It was early autumn. Dew sparkled in the grass like diamonds, but no one seemed to notice. Then Tom rode up beside me.

"Can you believe how lovely this morning is?" he asked. I smiled at him. This time I didn't look away.

Tom and I became friends. We rode horses, went for walks with his dogs, ate dinner together, and spent hours talking about Dick Francis's horse mystery novels. Before I knew it, I fell in love. But I didn't have the courage to ask Tom how he felt about me.

One day Tom told me he was moving to Florida for another job. I couldn't let him leave without telling him how I felt. But I couldn't tell him in person. I poured my heart out in a letter. "All my life I've waited for a man like you," I wrote, "a man who sets my mind at ease. I know God introduced us for a reason. We're meant to be together." Before I lost my courage, I put the letter inside a Dick Francis novel I'd borrowed from him. I left the book on his desk.

The next morning Tom stopped by while I was cleaning a stall. "Come by the house tonight."

True love in this differs from gold and clay That to divide is not to take away.
PERCY BYSSHE SHELLEY

That night I knocked at his front door. "Hi, Thirza," he said slowly. I had my answer. I heard it in his voice. He sat me down on his sofa. "I think it's best if we just stay friends," he said.

Tom left a few weeks later. Eventually I left Pin Oak myself, and enrolled at the University of Kentucky. I majored in middle school education and moved in with a friend, Nancy. "If I'm not going to have a relationship, at least I can have a career," I told her one night. She'd known Tom, too, and patiently listened to all my stories about him. I still thought about Tom, even three years after we said good-bye. Our friendship was the closest thing I'd ever had to a real romance.

One day, Nancy stormed into my room. "Thirza, you won't believe who I just ran into! Tom!" I could hardly move. "We talked, and he told me he was lonely." Nancy looked at me, scheming. "You know, he doesn't live that far away."

Tom's birthday was coming up. With present in hand, I went to his house. "Here I am again," I thought, "hoping Tom will love me back." I knocked on the door. "God, give me courage, like Jay Trump."

Love is the only force capable of transforming an enemy into a friend.

MARTIN LUTHER KING

"Thirza!" Tom said. I handed him the gift. "You remembered?" He opened the envelope. A smile came over his face as he pulled out a big photograph of Peaks and Valleys, who had gone on to become a champion racer.

Six years later, Tom and I are happily married. Like Jay Trump, I'm an unexpected winner— especially when it comes to trusting in love.

Two Men

MATTHEW VERNON

I t's a warm summer morning, about 4:45 A.M. School has just ended and I am enjoying my lazy summer sleep, but something stirs me from slumber. I pull the sheets close to my chest, but something ends the innocent sleep. It is my father. I hear him calling me from the door; his voice is strong yet quiet in his old age. He tries to be humorous, saying, "Come on, son, we're burning daylight." When I groan and don't respond, I feel the smile leave him, and it is replaced by a simple command, "Get up and be ready to leave in five minutes!" Then the door closes with a jolt, leaving me alone with the burden of the day at hand. I swing my legs out of bed and pull on my jeans, dreading every moment. I assure myself that there can be nothing worse than working construction with your father. Five minutes later I am in the kitchen getting coffee.

> *Of all earthly music that which reaches farthest into heaven is the beating of a truly loving heart.*
>
> HENRY WARD BEECHER

My dad, Ralph Vernon, lifetime construction worker with little more than a high school education, raises his balding head from the breakfast table after finishing his prayer, and fixes his hard green eyes upon me. There is silence. I collapse in my chair and slowly drink my coffee. I glance at him, and he smiles at me, holding that cracked and hardened forty-seven-year-old face out at me for some sort of inspection, and asks me if I would like to look at the plan for the day's job. I tell him I know my job: sweep, pack lumber, and stay out of the way when someone important comes. Once again the smile leaves, and we head off to the job. The ride is long and quiet, and I feel disgust building inside me for this insensitive slave driver.

I am lulled to sleep by the creaking and moaning of the old pickup that was my grandfather's, and has been my father's since Grandpa's death. It is my dad's prized possession, therefore, I hate it. Upon arrival at the job, I climb out of the old clunker

There are many in the world who are dying for a piece of bread, but there are many more dying for a little love.

MOTHER TERESA

with a distinct pout, and begin to set up the saws and cords needed for the day. We are finishing up preparations for an eight o'clock concrete pour, and even in the early morning fog I feel the sultry 100-degree heat the weatherman forecast the night before. Time passes quickly. I take my shirt off. As I perspire, I feel the dust

Where there is great love there are always miracles.

WILLA CATHER

stick to my body. I'll be glad when three-thirty comes.

At seven-thirty, our finishing touches are complete, and I relax and break for coffee while we wait for the concrete specialists to arrive. Eight o'clock comes and the tyrant is downright irritable. He says something about not being able to cancel the order of concrete, giving me a deliberate look. I grin at him. Just then we hear the sound of the cement mixer-trucks coming down the dusty road. Eighty yards of concrete (several thousand dollars worth)—and just me and my dad!

All at once we realize break is over and that we're in it all alone. I'm annoyed, to say the least. I pull my rubber gloves on and get ready to shovel "mud." My dad holds the chute and the water hose; the mixture must be perfect, especially in this weather. We begin on the two low walls, both set with two-by-six-foot forms. This goes smoothly; Dad is in total control. He places the chute perfectly and can gauge a yard of concrete just by feeling with his hands. I begin to wonder why we need specialists on this job anyway, as I do a quick, rough trowel of the lower sides. So far, we've completed thirty yards and four trucks, with about fifty yards and six trucks more to come—I realize this is a record-breaking pour. As the fifth truck is readied, we begin to pour the walls six feet high. This much con-crete puts a lot of pressure on the forms, and now our troubles begin. We have a blowout, and "mud" pours from the base. We have to stop the pump and push the bottom joint form onto the shoes (which hold them in place). As we strain together and are at last successful, I see a man I hadn't known in my father. The day was long and hard, with no room for any of my childish traits, and I managed to push them aside. Twelve hours later we sit down together and have coffee again.

When I was a boy of fourteen, my father was so ignorant I could hardly stand to have the old man around. But when I got to twenty-one, I was astonished how much the old man had learned in seven years.

MARK TWAIN

As we drive home in the sweet-sounding classic truck that had been my grandfather's and now is my dad's, the sun goes down around us. I think of our accomplishment: twelve hours, eighty yards, and tons of money. Something breaks through again. I feel the smile on my father's face, and I smile. Two men, father and son, both brimming with newfound pride, respect and love for each other. I lean back in the soft old seat, where my dad once felt the same feelings for his dad, and I sleep.

My Long Journey

GABRIEL ATEM

My friends and I had heard about the fighting. We heard that the Sudanese army would kill boys like us, boys from southern villages who might one day join rebels fighting for religious freedom. But the rumors didn't seem real—until the day soldiers came to my small villages.

I was only five years old. But I still remember. On that day, my friend and I played tag, running around our grass huts. My mother sang and stirred porridge over an open fire nearby.

A person needs just three things to be truly happy in this world. Someone to love, something to do, and something to hope for.

TOM BODETT

Suddenly, a shrill crack of machine-gun fire sounded through our quiet village. People screamed. "Run!" my friend yelled in our Dinka language. "Run into the jungle!"

More machine guns fired. Then soldiers appeared—Sudanese army soldiers. They moved quickly through our village, shooting people. I stumbled. Someone bumped into me, knocking me to the ground. A sea of legs and bodies blurred past me.

Where is my mother? Where is my father?

"Get up!" a tall boy shouted. He pulled me to my feet.

I had no time to think. The gunfire was too close. So I headed with this tall boy into the jungle.

We ran for an hour. Two hours. The further we got from my village, the more I worried about my family. Are they still alive? When I was too tired to go on, an older boy, Bashir, carried me on his back. Maybe a hundred of us ran together, on old trails cloaked by shrubs and towering trees. Finally, we rested in the tall grass of a savanna.

Do not ask the Lord for a life free from grief, instead ask for courage that endures.

AUTHOR UNKNOWN

"Can we go back?" I asked.

Bashir, still panting from running, shook his head no.

"Where are we going?" I asked.

Bashir pulled at the grass. "Ethiopia," he said finally. "We'll be safe there. But it's many, many miles. You must sleep."

We huddled together in the grass that night. But sleep was impossible. We jumped at every small noise, afraid it was the soldiers coming to capture us. My stomach growled with hunger and my throat was dry from thirst. I missed my mother so much! I cried and cried.

When the morning light arrived, Bashir touched my shoulder. "We must go."

We walked barefoot through the steamy jungle, which was filled with screeching birds and dark shadows. More and more boys who had fled from other villages joined us. Soon hundreds of boys were walking with us. As I trudged on, I tried to remember what my mother had told me. Only God knows what will happen in the future. If you ask, he will take you in his hands. So as I walked, I prayed.

> *And having thus chosen our course, let us renew our trust in God and go forward without fear and with manly hearts.*
>
> ABRAHAM LINCOLN

Each morning, I woke with the familiar ache of hunger. Bashir made a spear from bamboo, and we used it to hunt small animals. But it was hard to catch anything. Sometimes we ate grass and leaves—or even handfuls of yellow clay. Many boys simply lay down and died from starvation.

One morning, Bashir and I roamed deep into the jungle, looking for mangoes. Suddenly, from out of the tall grass, a lion pounced, grabbing Bashir by the chest. I froze, helpless. Sticks and rocks would be no match for this beast. *I can't save him*, I thought. *I have to get away!* Terrified, I scrambled back to the others, screaming. "Run! A lion! Run!"

Please God, I prayed as we tore through the jungle. *Please protect us.*

Three months after I fled my village, we reached the banks of the Gilo River, the river that separates Sudan and Ethiopia. It was an amazing sight. Thousands of boys like me were camped along the river, waiting until a boat or a raft was available to take them across to a refugee camp on the other side. Some worked on constructing their own rafts. Nobody wanted to swim across because the river was deep and wide—and full of crocodiles.

Tell me how much you know of the sufferings of your fellowmen, and I will tell you how much you have loved them.

HELMUT THIELICKE

One day we heard machine guns behind us in the distance. Word quickly spread: "The Sudanese army is approaching!" Then we heard the roar of trucks, and we knew we had to make a decision—bullets or crocodiles. Quickly, we waded into the Gilo.

Somehow I found a raft and hung on to it, paddling hard. All around me, boys disappeared, snatched by crocodiles or unable to swim. Those of us who made it across walked wearily to the refugee camp.

Two men stopped us at the gates. One of them seemed upset to see so many of us. "You've got to let them in," the bearded man wearing a United Nations uniform said. "Look at them! God knows how far they've walked. We can't turn them away!"

The bearded man turned to us and opened his arms wide. We had a new home. Later, I found out we'd walked more than 500 miles.

In the refugee camp, we lived in mud huts. We lay down each night on grass beds, ten in a hut. The smell of smoke and sweat—along with rasping coughs—made it difficult to sleep. Many of those who coughed didn't survive. Those long, dark nights were the hardest. I missed Bashir. I missed my friends from the village. I missed my parents and brothers and sisters.

The way to love anything is to realize that it might be lost.

G. K. CHESTERTON

Tabor, an older boy, guarded me from the draft of the open doorway on cold nights with his body. Except for Tabor, I had no one.

"Tabor," I said one night.

He raised his head.

"You are my friend," I said. "Thank you."

I had three birthdays at that refugee camp. It was now 1992. But on my eighth birthday, the U.N. people told us we had to move again. A new government in

Ethiopia had given the Sudanese soldiers approval to come get us. We all knew that meant certain death.

"We must go," Tabor said.

For the next three months, I walked with hundreds of others another 600 miles sough, through the jungle. Sometimes we passed small villages and people gave us corn to eat.

Finally, we arrived in Kakuma, Kenya, at a refugee camp of 60,000 people from eight different countries. I talked with many people from Rwanda who had also fled mass killings. Everyone at the camp had been chased from their country, fearing for their lives.

Life at the refugee camp was hard. There was no soap. No water. No electricity. Sometimes I headed down a long trail to a shallow, brownish lake several miles away to swim and bathe. When our daily ration of porridge wasn't enough, we searched the jungle for leaves to eat. At dusk, we returned with a sack of edible leaves to the only family we knew—one another.

The fingers of God touch your life when you touch a friend.
MARY DAWN HUGHES

Fortunately, we attended school each day, starting at 7:30 A.M. Inside a large grass hut, a teacher taught us science and math. Twenty of us shared one worn book. I wrote multiplication tables in the dry, red clay because we had no paper. We sang our "ABCs" to help us learn English.

One day, our teacher stood in front of our classroom. "I have something very important to tell you," he said. "Some of you will be able to go to America."

We sat in silence, stunned by the news. We all had heard about America in our studies.

Endurance is not just the ability to bear a hard thing, but to turn it into glory.

WILLIAM BARCLAY

"How well you learn English and how well you do your school-work will decide if you are chosen to go to America," the teacher said.

"I am going to work hard," I told Tabor. "I don't want to worry about soldiers coming ever again."

From that day on, I studied eagerly, especially English. Several months later, a man from the U.N. asked me questions about America. He asked me why I wanted to go there and what would I do if I got that chance.

"I would work hard!" I told him. "Please give me the opportunity."

"You're going to America," he said.

I cried with joy.

In January 2000, I took my first plane ride—to

Seattle, Washington, USA. It was the beginning of a new life.

I was seventeen, and I had never flipped on a light switch, never seen a television, never used a can opener or a fork. That first night, my new family opened the oven, pulled out a fragrant, flat, cheesy meal and said, "This is pizza." To me, it looked like heaven.

Now, for the first time since I was little, I have a family. I have parents who have taken me into their home. I call them Mom and Dad. I finally feel like I belong.

I have no pictures of my real parents. Only memories. I can see my father, Abrahm, and my mother, Amour, in my mind, but I don't know if they are alive. I've heard that my village no longer exists, that my people are scattered and there is still civil war. One day I hope to go back to Sudan, but not until there is peace.

Wherever you go, go with your whole heart.

CONFUCIUS

In spite of everything that has happened to me, I still believe what my mother told me. God has taken me in his hands—and he will keep me there.

The Power of Love at School

Home in America

MAJA RUZNIC

I swallowed hard and pushed open the door of the school. In my hand I clutched a slip of paper: *Grade: 7. Homeroom: 101. Teacher: Mr. Patton.* Kids were all around, laughing and shouting, saying things in English—a language I couldn't understand. *They're probably talking about me!* I thought. *They can tell I don't belong here.*

Love and kindness are never wasted. They always make a difference. They bless the one who receives them, and they bless you, the giver.

BARBARA DE ANGELIS

I wanted to turn around and get back on the bus. I wanted to go home. Home to Bosnia.

I was born in Bosnia, a country at war. Serbians, Croatians, and Bosnians, Bosnia's three ethnic groups, were killing each other over religion. I was eight years old when the war forced my family to flee across the river to Croatia, and then to a refugee camp in Austria. Other than the few clothes we could snatch off the clothesline as we ran from our home, we had to leave everything behind.

Once we got to the camp, we slept on cots in

an old church with other refugees. I made friends with the other kids and started school, where I learned German, the language spoken in Austria. We'd lived there only a few years when Mom began talking about going to the United States.

I didn't want to hear about America. Everything I knew about it came from the TV show *Beverly Hills, 90210*. I definitely wasn't going to fit into that world! Besides, I didn't want to learn another new language. The thought of moving again—all the way across the ocean—made me sick to my stomach.

But Mom was convinced that moving to the U.S. would be the opportunity of a lifetime. Even though I was young, she wanted me to be as excited about the idea as she was. So she kept working on me, talking to me at dinner, before bed, and in the morning as I was getting ready for school.

Love cures peoples—both the ones who give it and the ones who receive it.

KARL MENNINGER

"Maja, if we go, we'll have so many opportunities," she'd say. "There are people of all kinds there, and no fighting like in Bosnia. We'll be accepted for who we are. It may be difficult, but we'll build a better life."

"But I like my life here," I told her. "I like my

friends. And I can finally speak German. I just can't start all over."

"You did it here," Mom reminded me. "I know it was hard at first, but you got used to it."

Mom was right—it had been hard adjusting to life in Austria. Especially school, where a lot of the Austrian kids picked on us refugee students. But as the months passed, it had gotten easier. Now I was finally feeling comfortable.

Still, the way Mom talked about America made it sound . . . wonderful. And exciting. People of all kinds. No fighting. A better life.

Finally, the opportunity Mom had hoped for came. "The International Rescue Committee is sponsoring families," Mom told me one day. "Your aunt and uncle and cousins are already there. Now we have a chance to go!"

Love is life. All, everything that I understand, I understand only because I love.

LEO TOLSTOY

So that summer, Mom, my stepdad, my little sister, and I boarded a plane for San Francisco—the name written on the tab of my Levi's jeans.

Now, as I stood in the hallway of my new school, clutching my slip of paper, I wished I'd never gotten on that plane. I felt more scared than I had ever been in my entire life. More scared than I'd been those first weeks in the refugee camp. More scared than I'd been in Bosnia, when Mom and I had huddled in our neighbor's bomb shelter, air-raid sirens wailing.

"My name is Maja," I kept repeating to myself. It was the one English phrase I knew how to say.

I walked into an office where adults were sitting and held out my slip of paper to a woman sitting at the desk. She looked at it, said a bunch of words, then pointed to the door. *I don't know what she means!* But I nodded, pretending to understand, and went out the door. I was lost. No one spoke to me as I wandered up and down the halls.

Love is an act of endless forgiveness, a tender look which becomes a habit.

PETER USTINOV

Finally, I walked back into the office and held out my paper again, my face flushed with embarrassment.

"Do you speak English?" the woman asked. *Finally—some words I understand!* I shook my head.

She led me to a classroom full of students. Some were sitting, others walked around—one girl was even singing. I couldn't believe how loud it was.

I sat down at an empty desk. The girl in front of me turned around. "Hello," she said. "My name is Kamara."

I know how to answer! "My name is Maja," I said slowly, making sure I got the words right.

Kamara started saying something else. I saw her lips moving . . . but I couldn't understand. I shook my head to show that I didn't speak English. Kamara shrugged and turned back around. *I'll never make friends here!* I thought.

I went home that afternoon and cried. In the morning, I begged Mom not to make me go back to school.

Everything is, everything exists, only because I love. Everything is united by it alone.

LEO TOLSTOY

"Maja, I'm sorry, but you have to go," Mom said gently. "Sometimes we have to do things we don't want to. Sometimes that's the only way to get what we want in life."

The first few months of school were awful. I cried every night and woke up in the morning dreading each day. In Bosnia, I had been one of the better students. At school in America, I sat silently through classes while everyone around me laughed and talked. *I'm never going to fit in here.*

As the weeks went by, I started to understand what other kids were saying to me. More and more often, I could answer back. Slowly, things began to get better. Still, I missed life in Bosnia. I missed my old school, where I could talk in my native Serbo-

Croatian and not worry about getting the words mixed up. I missed Nana and Dedo, my grandparents, who were too old to make the journey to America with us. I longed for that time when I felt totally at home.

Then one day, I was sitting in the cafeteria with some other students when a boy threw a baseball our way. Instead of ducking, I jumped up and ran toward the ball, caught it, and threw it back. Cynthia, one of the girls I'd been sitting with, stared at me.

Bitterness imprisons life; love releases it.

HARRY EMERSON FOSDICK

"What?" I asked.

"You have a quick turn-around time," she said. "You should run track."

"What's track?" I asked. I'd never heard that word.

Cynthia laughed. "It's a bunch of people who get together to run. You know, compete in races. I'm going out for the team this year. You should do it, too."

Maybe this "track" is something I can do, I thought. *Something that will help me fit in.*

At tryouts, the coaches tested our speed and agility, putting us through various drills. "Okay, listen up," Coach Block announced, gesturing toward the street behind the school. "I want all of you to run around this block four times. The five girls who can do it the fastest will be on our long distance team. Remember—pace yourself!"

I took off at the coach's signal. As I rounded the first block, I glanced at the other runners beside and behind me. Some of them were getting winded already. *This feels so easy*, I thought. *It's like I was meant to do this.*

Bitterness paralyzes life; love empowers it.

HARRY EMERSON FOSDICK

I finished the fourth block at the head of the group, full of energy and adrenaline. "Maja, that was terrific," Coach said as he recorded my time on his clipboard. "You have great endurance and great speed—and that's something hard to find in a runner. You have a real future ahead of you!"

The future. Up until now, the future was something I'd dreaded. I'd been wrapped up in my past and all the things I'd had to leave behind. Now this coach was telling me I had something to look forward to here in America.

When our first track meet rolled around a few weeks later, I took my place alongside the other runners as they lined up for the 800-meter race. I looked down at my royal blue top, with my school's name, Everett, printed in block letters. *I can't believe I'm actually part of a team*, I thought. I took a deep breath to slow the butterflies that were churning in my stomach. *Okay, Maja*, I told myself. *Focus on winning.*

The gun went off—and the butterflies disappeared as my legs broke into a rhythm. My muscles tightened, but I pushed through the pain.

"Go, Maja! Go!"

People in the stands are calling my name!

"Go, Maja! Go!"

I didn't turn my head to see who it was. All I could think about was crossing the finish line. *One lap to go . . . half a lap . . . yes!*

I stormed across the finish line to the cheers of the crowd. I breathed hard, smiling as I walked around, hands on my hips, cooling down. *They were calling my name*, I thought. *Me—Maja Ruznic. The girl from Bosnia.*

Bitterness sickens life; love heals it. Bitterness blinds life; love anoints its eyes.

HARRY EMERSON FOSDICK

As my teammates and coaches came up to congratulate me, I knew I'd won more than an 800-meter race. I'd proven to myself that I belonged here. Here, in America.

A Night to Remember

AMY ELIZABETH CONNOR

I admit it. I wasn't blessed with perfect skin. From the moment that I turned thirteen, puberty kicked in with a vengeance. Almost overnight, my baby-face, peaches-and-cream complexion erupted into one gigantic source of inflamed misery that lasted for the rest of high school.

To love and be loved is to feel the sun from both sides.

DAVID VISCOTT

So when my senior prom— one of the most anticipated events of my high school career—finally rolled around, I was . . . dateless. I just knew that my breakouts were to blame. While the rest of my porcelain-skinned friends waltzed the night away at the Omni Hotel Royal Ballroom, I'd be stuck at home watching reruns with my parents.

Mom and Dad tried to sympathize. They prayed daily for my healing. I heard Romans 5 so many times that I had the entire passage memorized: "And we know that suffering produces perseverance; perseverance, character, and character, hope. And hope does not disappoint us. . . ."

"It'll pass, Liza, have patience," Mom kept

telling me. Sorry, but it was hard to be patient when each morning I'd rush to the mirror, hoping my day of redemption had come, only to be disappointed over and over and over.

Finally, the dreaded prom night arrived and the cruel theme was "A Night to Remember." To make matters worse, my baby sister had a date to the big dance, and she was only a freshman. That afternoon, I found myself with nothing to do but play hairstylist, makeup artist, and fashion consultant to my prom-bound sibling. Choking back tears, I halfheartedly wished her a good time as she slipped into the stretch limo. How she'd managed to sidestep the family "acne genes" was beyond me.

The first duty of love is to listen.

PAUL TILLICH

Once my sister was on her way, I settled on the couch with the TV remote control. I just wanted the night to be over.

Then the phone rang. It was Denise Cambell, our youth pastor's wife.

"Liza, you've got to help me," she begged. "My sitter bailed at the last minute. We're on our way out the door to the annual Sunday School Board Banquet. Can you please watch Caleb?"

The last thing I wanted to do was spend the evening entertaining a high-strung six-year-old, but when I heard the panic in Mrs. Cambell's voice, I couldn't say no.

I arrived at the Cambells' to find Caleb dressed in a cowboy hat and chaps, covered in fingerpaint.

Loving can cost a lot, but not loving always costs more.

MERLE SHAIN

"He's been painting a cardboard stable for his imaginary herd of mustangs," Mrs. Cambell explained. "Ever since we let him watch that old movie, *Tombstone*, he's been stuck in this Western phase."

"Thank you so much for filling in, Liza," she said, rushing out the door. "Oh, and there's dinner in the fridge . . . and bedtime is eight o'clock."

Just as the front door slammed, Caleb sauntered into the kitchen. He was dragging dirt and grass from the backyard on the heels of his oversized spurs.

"Watcha fixin' for supper, little lady? I'm one hungry cowboy," he declared matter-of-factly. I opened the fridge to find dinner—leftover spaghetti and grapes. *Just perfect*, I thought. While my friends were dining on prime rib, I was eating day-old spaghetti.

After supper, Caleb and I retreated to the play-room. He wanted to show me how to two-step. *How ironic*, I thought. *The rest of the girls my age are waltz-ing the evening away under a spinning disco ball in the arms of their dream dates. And here I am, two-stepping to a little boy wearing plastic holsters.*

The good thing is, by the time Caleb's bedtime rolled around, I had spent so much time playing cowboy that I managed to forget about my depressing prom situation. But as I tucked Caleb in bed, I was reminded of the reason that I was singing campfire lullabies instead of swaying to romantic love songs.

"Liza, what are those red spots on your face?" Caleb asked innocently as I stopped down to kiss him goodnight. My heart sank. How could I explain the misery of teenage acne to this smooth-skinned-six-year-old? Before I could respond, Caleb reached up, stroked my cheek, and declared in a soft western drawl, "I think they look beautiful on you, little lady."

His comment struck me as so funny that I just laughed out loud. As I gave him a goodnight hug, missing my senior prom didn't seem like such a big deal anymore. My heavenly Father, in his infinite wisdom, had used this little cowboy kid to remind me that I was beautiful. And that did more for my self-esteem than any over-rated, prom night fantasy ever could.

I love you not only for what you are, but for what I am when I am with you.

AUTHOR UNKNOWN

Prom Night

ADAM POPE

T hat sour medical odor hit me right as I stepped into the lobby of Mountain View Nursing Home. I was stuck there for an hour and a half with some of my friends. We call ourselves the Tippers because whenever we eat at one of the local hot spots—pizza at Yanni's, burgers at the Beacon or Billy D's—we leave behind more than our fair share. We try to be generous in other ways too, raising money for scholarships and volunteering in the community. One guy had the bright idea to "adopt" the patients living in one wing of the nursing home. "We'll make regular visits," he proposed, "not just on holidays." He organized a calendar, making sure a bunch of us would be there two nights a week. I signed up for Monday nights to get it over with first thing in the week.

I love you not only for what you have made of yourself, but for what you are making of me.

AUTHOR UNKNOWN

But now that I was there, I wondered if I was borderline crazy. What high school kid in his right mind would want to spend the night playing checkers and talking to some sick people when what he really wanted was to be at home watching Monday Night Football?

A nurse greeted my friends and me in the lobby. "The residents are looking forward to meeting you boys," she said. "Follow me." We walked down a long corridor with open doors, past blaring televisions, and people in wheelchairs. Some were dressed in ordinary clothes, but others wore pajamas, slippers, and bathrobes. Some leaned on their walkers and just stared out the window, like they thought angels would be coming down any minute to carry them up to heaven.

"Here's the activity room," said the nurse. The tables had cards or checkers laid out on them. *Big fun*, I thought. A burly guy in a wheelchair maneuvered over to us. "This is Barry," the nurse said. He muttered something out of the corner of his mouth and managed to raise his hand on the same side. The rest of his body was paralyzed. Another man steered toward me in his electric wheelchair. "Howdy," he said. "I'm Carl."

I shook his hand.

"The Tippers," he said. "Must be because you like to tip back and relax." He laughed at his joke. "I

> *Make new friends, but keep the old;*
> *One is silver, the other is gold.*
> JOSEPH PARRY

tip my hat to you." He raised his baseball cap, and we all laughed. You couldn't help it.

"I'm Sister," said a white-haired lady. "So nice of you boys to come visit." She was as gracious as if it were a fancy tea party and we were visiting royalty. I think she would have curtsied if she had not been in a wheelchair. "You kind gentlemen go ahead with your games. I'll just sit and chat."

I took a seat, and Barry gestured to the cards. "I'll deal," I said. There was a stack of red, white, and blue poker chips; I shuffled the deck. "The weather has been lovely this fall, don't you think?" said Sister.

"Yes, ma'am." I started dealing. Barry had a little plastic stand at his place, like one of those racks for Scrabble letters. I dealt his cards right into the rack.

One friend in a lifetime is much; two are many; three are hardly possible.

HENRY ADAMS

"Still, we could use a little rain," Sister went on. "How I love the smell of rain." *Yes, ma'am,* I thought. *I wish we had some rain right now.*

I watched my pile of chips diminish and Barry's rise, while Sister jumped artfully from topic to topic: music, gardening, TV programs. She seemed to have more interests than I had socks.

"Looks like you're having trouble there, son,"

Carl said. I was ready to cash in my last blue chip when we had to go. "Good game," I said. "Y'all come back now," Sister chimed in. "Or we'll come looking for you!" Carl called out. I realized something amazing: I hadn't thought once about Monday Night Football.

I went back week after week. Not that I ever grew fond of the disinfectant smell or the patients who stared out the windows. It's just when I was in the activity room playing games or chatting with Sister, I forgot what people were wearing, sitting in, or leaning on. I was too busy trying to beat Barry (I never came close), one-up Carl with a joke (he was always quicker), or charm Sister in friendly conversation.

> *Each friend represents a world in us, a world possibly not born until they arrive, and it is only by this meeting that a new world is born.*
>
> ANAIS NIN

As springtime approached, someone came up with the idea of having a prom with the residents of Mountain View. The idea won quick approval. The nurses scoured thrift shops for fancy dresses, and the men polished their lace-up shoes. *I'm going to a prom already*, I thought, *with my friend Jenny*. I was thinking I might even dance, if I didn't feel too embarrassed. I'd been saving and planning for weeks to make everything just right.

"Come on, Adam," my Tipper buddies told me. "You've got to do the prom at Mountain View too."

I agreed to go, but I'd keep it simple. I wore my blazer and bow tie and drove my pickup truck. Some girls we knew agreed to come and be dates for the men at the home. We were being paired up with residents from all the wings at Mountain View, not just "ours."

Corsage in hand, I went into the dining room. Every table was decorated with a floral centerpiece and balloons. Music was coming from the speakers— Glenn Miller and Frank Sinatra—and there was a dance floor in the center. *Won't be much dancing here with all those wheelchairs and walkers,* I thought. "Your date is Mrs. Parker," one of the nurses told me as she gestured to an attractive woman in a red dress with pearl earrings. A blind date! "Nice to meet you," I said. I slipped the corsage on her wrist and pushed her wheelchair over to a table with some friends and their dates. We had punch and cookies, and I wondered what to say next. Then I remembered Sister. "The weather has been beautiful," I remarked.

A righteous man is cautious in friendship.
PROVERBS 12:26

"It certainly has."

"Still, we could use some rain." Carl was holding court across the room with a group of kids around him laughing, naturally. Barry sat at a table with some of the high school girls. Probably wished he could play a hand of poker with 'em. Then I noticed Mrs. Parker's foot tapping the footrest of her wheelchair.

"Would you like to dance, Mrs. Parker?" I asked, offering my hand.

Her face lit up like a sparkler. "That would make my day!" she exclaimed. I wheeled her out on the dance floor, figuring I could push her around a little. But to my amazement she stood up, and took my hand. I practically had a heart attack. I looked over my shoulder, and one of the nurses nodded encouragingly. My buddies clapped their hands. I raised Mrs. Parker's hand slightly, and we took some tentative steps around the floor. Soon we both relaxed. My date danced like a dream, and she smiled at me as if I did too.

Friendship cheers like a sunbeam; charms like a good story; inspires like a brave leader; binds like a golden chain; guides like a heavenly vision.

NEWELL D. HILLIS

Later that month I took Jenny to our school prom. She wore a peach-colored dress and I gave her a corsage of sweetheart roses. She pinned a white boutonniere on my tux. We had filet mignon at the Piedmont Club, then danced at the cafeteria. Jenny assured me it was a night to remember. But I never forgot about all my friends back at Mountain View. Barry taught me how to improve my poker game, Sister taught me how to make conversation, Carl showed me how a joke can break the ice. And Mrs. Parker, my charming blind date, showed me how to dance.

Some of those people were waiting for angels to carry them up to heaven. But they were determined to laugh and dance and play—and teach a few new tricks to a high school kid like me—up until the last moment. Because they knew that when you give something of yourself to somebody else, you get more back than you ever bargained for.

What is a friend:
A single soul
dwelling in
two bodies.

ARISTOTLE

Royal Awakening

BETH KARKOSAK

*M*y sister was crowned homecoming queen when I was four years old. From that moment on, I dreamed of the day it would be my turn.

When my sister was away at college, I'd sneak into her closet and try on her crown. I'd envision myself walking onto the football field, a dozen red roses in my arms, waving at the crowd.

During my elementary years, I had lots of friends. My sister had been popular, so I figured that was the key to being voted homecoming queen. I was off to a good start. But as ninth grade approached, I became anxious. My parents had sent me to a private school for junior high. *Will they remember me?* I wondered. *Will I still be popular?* Boyne City High was a small, rural school—the kind of place where everybody knew everybody. And if you didn't fit in—well, you had a definite problem.

In my friend, I find a second self.

ISABEL NORTON

By late August, my mom got tired of me stressing over what to wear the first day. "Beth, why don't you make a list of personal goals," she said. "Things you want to accomplish in high school."

"M-o-o-o-m!" I whined.

Half an hour later, I handed her a list of six items. She looked it over and hugged me. "High school is a confusing time, Beth," she said, placing the list in my "baby keepsakes" box. "If you lose track of who you are or what your priorities are, this will remind you."

Stay is a charming word in a friend's vocabulary.

LOUISA MAY ALCOTT

On the first day of school, my worst fears came true. My old friends had made new friends, and they treated me like an outcast. All one-hundred freshmen had either forgotten who I was, or they remembered and didn't care.

Make that ninety-nine. There was one girl who was nice to me—Maureen. She was smart and friendly, and she wasn't afraid to be herself.

"You're just jealous!" she said to a group of girls who muttered insults as they passed. "Don't let them bug you, Beth. They think they're cool, but they're not."

Problem was, I thought those girls were cool, and I wished I were one of them. They dressed in Abercrombie clothes and went to parties. They dated boys who were snowboarders, skiers, and football players. *At this rate, I'm never going to be popular, much less homecoming queen,* I thought.

Then one day, Maureen and I passed some upper classmen in the hall.

"Fresh meat," one guy jabbed his friend.

Maureen was incensed by their crude comments, but I didn't mind. *Maybe if I play along, I can be popular after all.*

"Hi," I smirked, rolling my eyes.

Two months later, Maureen and I were sitting together at a football game when the most popular sophomore guy in the school plunked down between us.

One's friends are that part of the human race with which one can be human.

GEORGE SANTAYANA

"Get lost, Craig," Maureen told him.

"Settle down, girl. I'm here to welcome Beth to our fine school," he said.

"Thanks," I smiled.

I got up and took a walk with him. An hour later, when we got back, Maureen was gone. *It's for the best,* I thought. Maureen didn't even try to be cool. Hanging with her was holding me back.

Craig took me to parties, and my popularity skyrocketed. I'd always said I wouldn't drink but my resolve crumbled after just one party. I drank and smoked like everyone else, just to fit in.

A week into tenth grade, Craig and I broke up. When word got out, Derrick, a junior, asked me to the homecoming dance. I shook my head and told him my parents were old-fashioned control freaks who wouldn't let me date until I was sixteen. He nodded knowingly.

"No problem," he smiled.

I liked his laid-back attitude.

What is a friend?
It is a person with
whom you dare
to be yourself.
FRANK CRANE

The next day, he handed me a note between classes. I took it to study hall and laughed out loud when I read the typed heading: "Ten Reasons Why You Should Go to Homecoming with Me." Who could resist that? Whatever it took, I was going with him.

It took a lot of lying. I told my parents that a group of us were going to the dance, not as dates, just as friends. "And then the girls are going to spend the night at Jen's so we can talk all night long!"

At the dance, Jen and her boyfriend got into a fight. She wanted me to go home early with her. "Don't leave, Beth," Derrick pleaded. "Let's go party and then I'll drop you off at Jen's later."

When I still hadn't arrived at Jen's by 3:00 A.M., her mother freaked and called my mother. A half-hour later I freaked when I saw my mom's car in Jen's driveway. Mom drove me home in silence—and the next day she grounded me for two months.

Back at school, Derrick treated me like an after-thought. He sat with his friends at lunch, bragging about how wasted he'd gotten the night before. Finally he came over to my table and asked how much longer I was grounded.

"I want us to be closer, Beth," he told me. "I want to really know you."

Finally, the grounding was over. I was getting tired of all Derrick's par-tying, but I stayed with him because everyone loved him. Being his girl-friend was the key to my popularity.

Your friend is the man who knows all about you, and still likes you.

ELBERT HUBBARD

During Christmas break my parents asked me to stick around home. I didn't put up much of a fuss—it was actu-ally nice to take a break. That week, I felt more alive. In a burst of energy, I decided to clean my room, top to bottom. When I got to my desk, I paged through a stack of old homework and exams. *I used to be an A student,* I thought. *Now I'm doing well to bring home Cs.*

Eyeing my baby box under my bed, I plopped down cross-legged on the floor and pulled it to me. "My Goals in High School." I read my old list slowly. "Get straight As" . . . "Have people respect me and my morals" . . . "Be a good example." With my finger, I traced where I'd signed "Beth." *Have I become someone else?*

My five brothers and sisters came home for New Year's Eve, and as usual we went to church together, ate shrimp, and waited for the ball to drop. Shortly after we turned on the TV, the doorbell rang.

It was Derrick. "Hey, there's an awesome party going on at Randy's! Let's go!"

"No, thanks," I said, walking him to his car. The snow squeaked under my boots, and the moon cast blue shadows on the ground.

Friendship, a dear balm . . . A smile among dark frowns: a beloved light: A solitude, a refuge, a delight.

PERCY BYSSHE SHELLEY

"Your parents still won't let you go?" he asked impatiently. "When are we ever going to be together, Beth? I know a nice place where we can be alone. It'll be really special. . . ."

"Derrick, you want something that I'm not willing to give," I said.

"Think it over, Beth," he said, touching my cheek. Then he drove away.

Back in the house, my family was making resolutions. Eat healthy, exercise more, lose weight—the usual stuff.

"Hey, Beth, what are you going to do?" my sister asked.

"I'm going to be a better person," I said. "And focus more on school." I saw relief in my parents' faces.

That night in bed, I thought about how complicated life had become. I'd pretended to be a party girl just to be popular. I'd lost my parents' trust, ruined my grade point average, and trashed old friendships.

I looked at the clock: 12:30. New Year's was for starting over. "God," I prayed. "I've made a mess of my life. Please show me how to get it back on track."

When I awoke the next day, I felt strong and clear about what I needed to do. I went right over to Derrick's, and I broke up with him. I cried all the way home. I knew I'd done the right thing, but it was hard.

> *The individual who thinks well of you, who keeps his mind on your good qualities, and does not look for flaws, is your friend.*
>
> ELBERT HUBBARD

Back at school, friends invited me to parties.

"Thanks, but I gave up partying," I said.

The first few times, they waited a few seconds, like they were expecting me to laugh and say, "Just kidding. Where's the party?" But I didn't. They'd shake their heads and walk away, confused.

The next few weeks, I felt so alone. More than anything I wanted to hang out with people who didn't need to party to have a good time. Like Maureen. We used to sleep over at one another's houses and talk on the phone for hours. Before I got "cool."

I finally got my courage up and called her.

"Maureen, it's me, Beth."

Silence. "Beth?"

No man is the whole of himself; his friends are the rest of him.

HARRY EMERSON

"I just wanted to tell you I'm sorry for being such a lousy friend. I was trying so hard to be popular that I forgot what's really important, like true friends. . . ."

"You used me between boyfriends, Beth. How do I know you won't do that again?"

"You don't."

Maureen paused. "Okay, well, maybe we can rent a video and you can sleep over this weekend."

I could barely contain my joy. *Thank you, God. Thank you for friends like Maureen.*

Junior year came and went, and I made more new friends—genuine friends. I had more fun than I'd ever had with the party crowd.

One morning the fall of my senior year, they passed out ballots for the Homecoming Court. As I circled a few names from among the whole senior class, I had to shake my head. *That old homecoming queen dream seems so shallow now,* I thought. *Getting good grades, building solid friendships, being honest and dependable—there's so much more that's really important.*

The day they announced the five girls and five guys who made the court, our P.A. system was down, so our teacher read the announcement aloud. "The 2001 Homecoming Court members are . . ." I doodled on my paper, only half-listening.

" . . . and Beth Karkosak!" I looked up. Was that my name? My friends shot out of their desks and came over and hugged me. The "cool" people stayed glued to their seats. They didn't look so cool to me anymore. They just looked tired and bored.

The day of the big homecoming game, I walked out onto the football field with the rest of the court.

"And the 2001 Homecoming Queen is . . ."

A hush came over the crowd.

" . . . Carrie Jones!"

What can give us more joy than a friend? Even more, is there something we need more?

DESIDERIUS ERASMUS

That's right, I didn't get crowned queen. But it didn't make one bit of difference. I bent to receive my runner-up crown, then waved to my friends in the stands. It wasn't the scene I'd imagined as a child, but somehow it was even better.

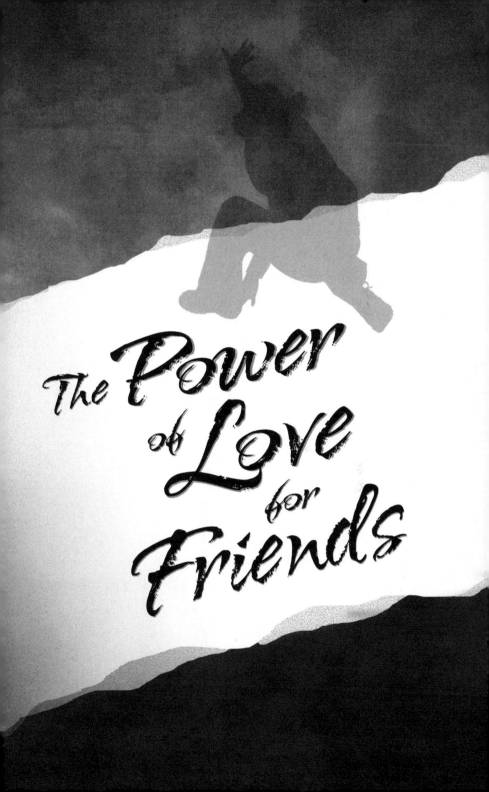

Soldier!

MARY H. HAINES

*W*hen I enlisted in the army, I was sent to Fort Jackson, South Carolina, for basic training. There, all of us recruits were assigned partners. "For the next eight weeks," the drill instructor told us, "your buddy is your best friend. Rely on her when you're in trouble." I was five foot five and pretty tough. I looked down at my partner: Monica Vallejo, a slender, four foot ten teenager from Arizona. *How could she ever help me?* I wondered.

The reward of friendship is itself. The man who hopes for anything else does not understand what true friendship is.

AILRED RIEVAULX

Basic was grueling, never-ending work. It became doubly hard when I caught the flu. But that didn't excuse me from drills. When I had trouble keeping up on our daily runs, Monica hung back by my side, encouraging me, telling me, "You can do it." One morning I awoke to find four loads of my laundry clean and neatly folded on top of my footlocker. Monica had washed it. "We're supposed to help each other," she said.

A couple of days later we marched fourteen miles in the scorching sun to a rifle range for practice. By the time we finished, moonlight shone through a cloud-filled sky. Only the reflector tape on the back of Monica's helmet kept me in line behind her on the return trek. The pace was steady, never picking up, never slowing down. My ankles swelled in my boots, and my legs screamed with every step.

Three miles to go. In the darkness I heard Monica's labored breaths. I knew she was in trouble. Maybe she wouldn't have been so tired if she hadn't spent all her free time helping me while I was sick. God, *how can I help her now?*

Moving a little closer behind her, I placed my hand beneath her twenty-pound backpack and gently lifted it, relieving her of some of its weight. With every bit of strength I could muster, I concentrated on holding up that backpack.

As the lights of the barracks came into view, I resumed my marching position at the proper distance and allowed Monica to take the last steps alone. We stored our gear in the wall lockers.

> *The most I can do for my friend is simply to be his friend. If he knows that I am happy in loving him, he will want no other reward. Is not friendship divine in this?*
>
> HENRY DAVID THOREAU

Lights went out. I climbed up to my bunk and collapsed onto my cool, clean sheets. In the quiet of the barracks, Monica called softly to me from the bunk below.

He prayeth best who loveth best all things both great and small.

SAMUEL TAYLOR COLERIDGE

"Mary," Monica whispered. "I knew I was ready to fall out tonight, so I asked God to help me with my load. Suddenly my back-pack felt lighter. God really heard my prayer."

And I knew he had heard mine too.

The Friendship Factor

SCOTT RUSSELL

I sorted through the stack of boxes on my bed. *Someone needs to outlaw moving twice in six months*, I thought. But I had to admit that part of me was glad for another change. We'd been living in a small town where everyone already knew each other and didn't seem to want extra company. I was on the outside of every conversation and was picked last in every game. Socially, my life needed some major work. In other words, I needed friends.

A true friend is like the refrain of a beautiful song.

F. PATARCA

I'll empty these boxes later, I told myself. *Time to check out the neighbors.*

There were only seven houses on our stretch of highway in rural Indiana, and ours was right in the middle. Stepping out the back door, I saw a cornfield. And out the front . . . a cornfield. I'm never going to make any friends around here, I thought.

My parents were already next door talking to the neighbors on our right. I walked over to join them.

A woman and her daughter stood on the back

patio. The mother called out to me. "Hey! Another guy on the block! Ricky will be so glad to meet you!" She yelled into the house, "Ricky! Come out and meet the neighbors!"

A moment later, Ricky stepped out.

"Look, Ricky!" his mother said. "There's another guy on the block!"

Ricky shifted his weight from side to side, his mouth a broad, open smile. He was a little shorter than I, and his legs didn't seem to bend at the knees. He stared at me through thick glasses, making these high-pitched squeaks as he breathed.

What's wrong with him?

Nothing can come between true friends.

EURIPIDES

"He wants to show you his Nintendo," his mother said.

My shoulders drooped. *Won't hurt me to be nice*, I thought.

I followed Ricky and his over-sized grin inside the house and into his small bedroom. Piles of stuff covered every piece of furniture—the desk, the set of shelves, the entertainment center. He plopped down onto his waterbed, then, leaning forward, reached out and tapped a curled hand on his Nintendo system.

"Hey, that's cool," I said.

Ricky stood and proceeded to tap other things

in the cluttered room with huge, sweeping motions. He showed me all his hats, shirts, vacation souvenirs, picture albums, birthday cards, and CDs—one by one. I smiled politely and nodded at each thing. But after about twenty minutes, I needed a break.

"Well, it's nice knowing there's someone my own age in the neighborhood," I said, trying to wrap up our visit.

"Ihn iegn-eegh," Ricky said.

"You're fifteen?"

"Ihn iegn-eegh."

"You're sixteen?"

"Ohn, lihhn . . . iiiegn . . . eeeeeeegn!"

"Thirteen?"

No matter where we are, we need those friends who trudge across from their neighborhoods to ours.

STEPHEN PETERS

Ricky grimaced. He placed the index finger of his right hand underneath his lower lip and brought it up to meet the top lip. I realized he couldn't close his jaw.

"Iiiiiim thhhhiiiieeeenthhteeeenthhhh."

"You're nineteen!"

"Uhh-huhh!" he said, nodding yes. "Iiigh erahchhuaeheh eraagh ear."

This was going to be a challenge. "Say that again, Ricky."

Again, he put his finger under his lip. "Iigh ger-ahchhuathdedth thleraaghth ear."

"Well, that's cool, Ricky. I bet you're proud to have graduated last year."

"Uhh huhh." He tapped his high school diploma hanging on the wall. "Iiign aaerehh ehh."

I smiled, hoping a nod would be the right response. In the half-hour since meeting Ricky, I had seen his room and translated two sentences, and my head hurt.

"Want to play Nintendo?" I asked, trying to change the subject—whatever the subject was.

Ricky raised his eyebrows, as if the thought had never occurred to him. He hobbled over to the gaming unit and pushed the reset switch. He waited. Nothing happened. He eventually realized his mistake and pushed another switch, turning the unit on. He handed me a controller as I sat down on the bed next to him, and we played for an hour. Ricky wasn't the greatest player, but he did a lot better than I expected.

We are not primarily put on the earth to see through one another, but to see one another through.

PETER DEVRIES

Over the next few weeks, I made a point of looking for friends in our new town. After this last move, I thought things might be different for me. But I was wrong. I was being home-schooled, so I didn't have too many opportunities to meet other kids my age. At our new church, I tried attending youth group, but nobody even said hello to me. It was like I had a "reject me" sign in glowing neon letters on my forehead. So I just sat there in a corner, with everyone ignoring me. *Why did I think people would treat me any differently here?* I thought. I decided to give up on my friend-finding mission.

I found myself coming back to visit Ricky every couple days. Life in our house in the cornfields was unbelievably dull, so I had a lot of time on my hands. Plus, I didn't own a Nintendo.

Nintendo turned out to be a great thing for both of us. I enjoyed playing. Ricky obviously couldn't make small talk, but he could move a joystick pretty well. I started going over to Ricky's house more and more.

One day after school, Ricky's mom filled me in on his disability. When he was eight, he'd been diagnosed

> *The glory of friendship is not the outstretched hand, nor the kindly smile nor the joy of companionship; it is the spirited inspiration that comes to one when he discovers that someone else believes in him and is willing to trust him with his friendship.*
>
> RALPH WALDO EMERSON

with the same disease his father had died from, Huntington's chorea. Basically, his brain cells were dying, which meant he was slowly losing control of himself, both mentally and physically. "There's no cure," she said. "The doctors told us he'd probably die before he graduated from high school."

"Well, he proved them wrong about that!" I said. "Maybe he's got a chance. . . ." Ricky's mom sighed and shook her head.

I hated to think of Ricky dying, losing control of his mind and body like that. Looking at his mom, I realized that Ricky was more than my Nintendo partner. He was becoming my friend.

One can do without people, but one has need of a friend.

CHINESE PROVERB

"Ricky's friends stood by him, all the way through school," his mom told me. "They voted him homecoming king his senior year. The local news even did a feature story on Ricky and his friends' support."

"So where are they now?" I demanded.

"His friends? Most of them are away at college," she said. "Ricky was left alone."

Alone. I knew all about alone.

After that, Ricky and I became closer. We played Nintendo, we watched TV, we talked about stuff that was going on with me at school.

Eventually, it got easier for me to understand his garbled speech. I could see why his classmates had stuck by him. He loved people. Soon, I wasn't just his friend—he was mine. Still, I couldn't help wishing for other friends, too.

Ricky started inviting me to what he called "Bible study" on Thursday evenings at the high school. I didn't see any reason to go. It didn't seem like the social scene I was looking for. People would probably just ignore me, as usual. But Ricky wouldn't let up.

Friendship is a sheltering tree.

SAMUEL TAYLOR COLERIDGE

"Okay, I'll go just once," I told him.

Ricky smiled his huge smile and gave me a high five.

When I got to Bible study, I found Ricky had invited me to a Campus Life club meeting. There were about fifteen teens there, both girls and guys. Everyone, from the freshmen all the way up to the seniors, made me feel welcome. I knew right away that I was going to make a lot of friends. And that's exactly what happened.

When I needed friends, God sent me Ricky. I was disappointed at first, but it was Ricky who showed me how to be a great friend. And once you've learned that, more friends are sure to follow.

Mamie

BONNIE BRIGHTMAN

I met Mamie through my friend, Ruby Dawn. Our school, Cole Christian, makes us do thirty hours of community service every year. The end of the year was coming fast, and I hadn't done any.

"Join the Little Buddies with me!" Ruby Dawn urged. This was a program that matched kids with older folks who needed a little help.

"Too risky," I said. "What if somebody keels over?"

"They won't," she insisted. "You'll see, Bonnie. It's fun!"

A friend is the one who comes in when the whole world has gone out.

GRACE PULPIT

So I became a Little Buddy and was matched up with Mamie, an eighty-two-year-old woman who lived alone in a trailer park for seniors. I was to visit Mamie whenever I could and make sure she was okay. And if she needed anything, all I had to do was call the Little Buddy social worker. That's it.

Since I needed a lot of service hours, and I needed them fast, it was I and Mamie and a Scrabble board nearly every afternoon for a month. I figured I'd finish up my thirty hours the week before school got out, which would give me afternoons free to hit the beach.

"What's that?" I asked, when Mamie tried to sneak by with the word *sortie* during our first game. Just because she was eighty-two didn't mean I was going to let her get away with anything.

A friend is one who walks in when the rest of the world walks out.

WALTER WINCHELL

"Well, a sortie is a bombing run made by an airplane," Mamie explained.

"Not allowed. It's French!" I insisted.

"Oh, you're quite right," Mamie replied graciously, removing the forbidden tiles. She paused, then carefully turned my word, *stab*, into *stabilizer*. This lady was out to win.

I eyed her suspiciously.

"It's a flap on an airplane that stabilizes and elevates the tail," she said. "Thirty-six points," she added. "Let's see you beat that."

I couldn't.

After a few more aeronautical terms made their way onto the board, I asked, "Were you a stewardess or something?"

Mamie laughed. "No. Nothing as glamorous. I was a pilot during World War II." So that photograph on the desk behind me was she! It showed a young woman standing underneath the wings of a biplane, holding a helmet in one hand, her hair blown back by the wind.

"They didn't trust women in combat, of course," Mamie said, recalling the war years one afternoon. She laid out a word on the Scrabble board. "But, you know, some of the flights we made were nearly as dangerous. Don't forget I had a double-letter score there!" she added, tapping the board sharply.

"I got it," I said.

"We had to make sure the planes were ready for combat, and sometimes they weren't. Thirty-eight women pilots died in service to our country."

I count myself
in nothing else
so happy
As in a soul
remembering my
good friends.
WILLIAM SHAKESPEARE

At some point, I forgot about the school's requirement and began looking forward to my Little Buddy visits. I liked hearing about those women pilots who'd had so much spirit. And I liked the spirit that Mamie still had.

Mamie must have enjoyed those visits, too, because she put a spare key outside on the porch under her geranium for me. That way, if she didn't answer the door, I could let myself in. One day, when she didn't answer, I found her at the kitchen table, her head resting on her arms. The kettle on the stove was boiling furiously. She had gotten a bit dizzy, she said.

When the weather was good, we'd stroll down to the beach. "Did you work for an airline after the war?" I asked once, as we sat in the sand and looked out at the water.

May the hinges of our friendship never rust.

AUTHOR UNKNOWN

Mamie shook her head. "No, no. That wasn't possible then. No one would hire a woman. Fortunately, my husband, Nick, was a pilot, too. We started our own little airline, flying tourists and hunters into the mountains north of here. It was a good life. When you fly, you're free." Mamie picked up a handful of sand and let it run through her fingers. "Nick's been gone twenty years now."

"Did he teach you to fly?" I asked.

"No. My dad taught me. We used to fly a small, red biplane in air shows in the Midwest."

I wondered how it would feel to break free of the earth like that. "It must have been scary the first time you went up."

"No, it wasn't—not with my dad there. The first time I took up a B-17 bomber, though, my teeth were chattering." Then Mamie yawned. "Sorry," she said. "This new medication tires me out." We walked slowly back to the trailer.

"Flying a B-17 was like trying to fly a football stadium," she said, as I helped her get comfortable on the couch and put an afghan over her feet.

"Mamie," I asked, "have you ever been afraid of anything?" But Mamie was asleep. I closed the door quietly behind me.

I had a creepy feeling the next day as I arrived at her trailer. When Mamie didn't answer the door, my knees got wobbly. I could smell smoke. Then, the smoke alarm started blasting its shrill scream.

Without friends, the world is but a wilderness.

AUTHOR UNKNOWN

"Mamie!" I called out. "Open up!" I knocked over the geranium plant, grabbed for the key, and burst in. Mamie was sleeping on the couch. Smoke was coming from the kitchen.

My hands shook as I reached for the fire extinguisher next to the stove. Mamie had left something cooking in the frying pan. It had spattered onto the burner and had caught a towel on fire. I got the fire out with a few blasts of the extinguisher, then reached up and shut off the alarm. I opened the windows and both doors to clear the smoke.

"Mamie, wake up!" I shouted, shaking her. She opened her eyes and jumped up from the couch.

"The porch," she said. "Get to the porch!"

We perched on the edge of the folding chairs until the smoke inside cleared.

Later, Mamie sat at the kitchen table stirring the tea I made for her. We hadn't said a word since we'd come inside.

"Are you going to tell the social worker?" she asked.

"Should I?"

"They'll make me go into a nursing home, you know." Her voice quavered.

I used ammonia to wash the soot off the wall behind the stove. *So this is what she fears—losing her freedom. Will I be the one who takes it away?* I felt a little sick.

"Do you think it's the medica-tion, Mamie?"

"I imagine so," she said. Her voice was steady now.

"Do you have to take it?"

What is the opposite of two? A lonely me, a lonely you.

RICHARD WILBUR

Mamie flicked some ash off her sleeve. "Yes. And the doctor says I'll have to take even more eventually. The side effects—the dizziness and fatigue—could get worse."

"Have you had any fires before, Mamie?" I asked, thinking about the time I'd found her with the kettle boiling out of control.

Mamie didn't answer.

That evening at the school basketball game, I told Ruby Dawn what had happened.

"You know what you have to do," she said.

"If I do, they'll put her in a nursing home," I shouted above the noise.

"If you don't, she's going to burn the place down!" Ruby Dawn yelled back.

That night, I prayed for guidance. In the morning, I made the call.

If you have one true friend, you have more than your share.

THOMAS FULLER

The social worker was a model of efficiency. Within two weeks, she had Mamie out of her trailer and into a nursing home.

The day they moved Mamie, I stood outside in the rain, watching. I'd tried to talk to her, but she wouldn't let me in when I came to the door, and the key was gone from under the geranium. She wouldn't talk to me on the phone, either. And now, when I called out to her, she wouldn't even look at me.

Ruby Dawn assured me it would all work out.

"Ziggy likes his nursing home," she said. She was Ziggy's Little Buddy.

"Ziggy's not Mamie," I said miserably.

I timed my visit to the nursing home so that Mamie would be on the patio when I got there. I spread the Scrabble board out on the little table next to her and sat down. I dug out some tiles and placed them across the board. *Forgive me.*

Think where man's glory most begins and ends, and say my glory was I had such friends.

WILLIAM BUTLER YEATS

Mamie looked at the words, and then she looked at me.

"You were right, of course," she said softly, as she took my hand in hers.

That night, I slept well for the first time since the fire. I still remember the dream I had. It was of a small, red, biplane flying free—looping about in a wide, blue sky.

Promises Never Die

JOAN GURLEY

It started with a promise. A promise I never thought I'd have to keep. I wanted to be a hairdresser and had a natural talent for it. Friends constantly asked me to cut their hair and apply their makeup. I really loved helping them look their best.

One day my best friend, Sandy, said, "If I ever die, promise you'll do my hair and make-up for me." She tossed her sun-streaked blond hair back and smiled like an imp. She was so full of energy, I couldn't imagine a time when she wouldn't be alive.

A friend is someone you can do nothing with and enjoy it.

AUTHOR UNKNOWN

"Promise, you won't let me look ugly in my coffin," she insisted.

I knew she wouldn't die for a long time, so I didn't give it a second thought. "Yeah, I promise." At eighteen, I figured we had plenty of time ahead of us.

That summer, my parents left for a tour of the Holy Land, and I got to stay at Sandy's house for a few weeks. I was always at Sandy's house anyway. Her mom called me her fourth child.

On the fourth of July, Sandy and I sat on the roof, watching fireworks. We watched the brilliant colors in the dark sky cascade back down to earth like waterfalls of light.

"Do you ever feel like that?" Sandy asked.

"Like what?"

"Like fireworks. One minute we explode brightly in the sky. The next minute we fade into nothing." Sandy touched my hand. "Promise me, Joan, you'll take care of me when I die."

We can do not great things; only small things with great love.

MOTHER TERESA

I didn't want to think such depressing thoughts, so I promised her again. "Sure, Sandy. No problem."

Three days later, while Sandy was out in her car, she hit another car in the grocery store parking lot—nicked it, really. But she bumped her head and chipped a tooth. She was upset and kept blaming herself. "If only I'd been more careful, this would never have happened. I shouldn't have had the radio on. I was going too fast."

Mrs. Reid hugged her daughter. "Don't worry about it, honey. Just be more careful next time. I'm just glad you weren't hurt."

Sandy brightened a bit. "Hey, Joan, let's see

how many friends we can visit today," she said, wriggling out of her mother's embrace. "I feel like getting outside of myself. I'm kind of down—probably because of the accident." She tossed me the keys to her car. "You drive. I don't feel like it."

I thought it was kind of odd to try to visit all of our friends in one afternoon. Still, I didn't have anything better to do.

> *Friendship is unnecessary, like philosophy, like art. It has no survival value; rather it is one of those things that give value to survival.*
>
> C. S. LEWIS

By late afternoon, we had visited just about everyone. After we'd seen the last friend, Sandy leaned back in her seat. "I don't feel good," she said. She looked kind of pale. "I want to go home and take a nap."

I figured she was just worn-out from the accident and all the running around we'd done. I dropped Sandy off at her house and then headed for my job at the jewelry store in the mall.

I got the call at work, around 6:00 P.M. It was Sandy's mom. "Sandy's gone," she said. "She lay down for a nap . . . and never got up." Then she broke down, sobbing.

"No, no! It can't be! I was with her all day. She was alive just a few hours ago!" *Sandy must be playing a trick. She's just pretending not to wake up*, I thought. But I knew Sandy would never do that to her mom. It had to be true. Sandy was dead. *What am I going to do without Sandy? How can I live without her?*

Then I remembered the promise. A burning filled my chest. Not panic or fear—it was a passionate desire to keep my promise. But could I really do it? More than anything in the world I wanted to be with Sandy. I needed to be close to her a while longer. But how could I explain that to Sandy's mom? I was afraid she'd think I was weird for wanting to be with a dead person.

True friendship is a plant of slow growth.

GEORGE WASHINGTON

When I got back to the house, Sandy's body had already been taken away. "Joan, would you go to the funeral home with me—to help me make the arrangements?" Mrs. Reid asked me, tears flowing from her eyes as she squeezed my hand.

"Of course I'll come," I answered, even though part of me didn't want to go.

At the funeral home, Sandy's mom talked to the people in charge. While she was busy with them, a powerful feeling came over me. I had to go down into the basement! Normally, I'd never have done anything like that. It would have been like a scene in a scary movie. But I moved ahead, as though in a dream.

I excused myself and headed for the stairs. At the bottom, I opened a door and went inside. The room was so cold it was like walking into a giant refrigerator.

That's when I saw Sandy. She was lying on her back on a metal table, covered up to her chin with a sheet. Someone must have just washed her hair, because she wore a cap dryer that was humming.

Love is blind; friendship closes its eyes.

AUTHOR UNKNOWN

The plastic cap covered her entire face, but I knew it was Sandy.

Suddenly I was outraged. Somebody had just stuck the dryer on my best friend like she was a thing, like she wasn't a person anymore and it didn't matter. I switched the dryer off and pulled off the cap. That's when I saw the awful things they had done to her face and hair.

Sandy had always worn a bob-style haircut, and her favorite lipstick was a pale pink. The funeral home people had given her a curly hairstyle and a bright-red lipstick. That was not Sandy!

I looked at the closed eyes of my friend's unfamiliar face. "It's a good thing I came down here, Sandy," I told her, as if she could hear me. I knew exactly how she did everything. I always sat in the bathroom talking with her while she did her makeup and hair. "Don't worry. I'm going to make you look beautiful."

I took a deep breath and asked God to help me fulfill my promise to Sandy. I suddenly felt strong. I didn't care anymore if her mother thought I was strange. I went upstairs and pulled Mrs. Reid aside.

Friendship multiplies the good of life and divides the evil.

BALTASAR GRACIAN

"I . . . I just saw Sandy," I told her. "They're not doing it right, Mrs. Reid," I said nervously.

"What—"

"Sandy doesn't look like herself. Her hair's all curly and her makeup is all wrong. Let me fix her up, Mrs. Reid. I know how to make Sandy beautiful again."

"Well, I guess . . . " Mrs. Reid answered. Then she paused and her face changed. It was as though she suddenly knew exactly how she wanted Sandy's farewell to her family and friends to be. Mrs. Reid told the funeral home director to let me do Sandy's hair and makeup. She gave me the keys to her car and asked me to bring back a dress for Sandy to wear for her funeral.

It was strange going into Sandy's room, knowing

she'd never be there again. I felt like a trespasser going through her things. With Sandy's makeup and her favorite dress, the lime green one with pink daisies, I headed back to the funeral home.

Sandy's hair was still damp, so I used a blow-dryer to get the curl out, brushing until it was sleek, just the way Sandy liked it. I care-fully drew eyeliner across each eye-lid. Then I brushed mascara on her long lashes. Finally, I took the red off her lips and put on her pale-pink shade. I was surprised at how hard and cold her skin felt, like white marble. But she looked like the Sandy I knew.

Friends are relatives you make for yourself.

EUSTACHE DESCHAMPS

After I finished, I felt relieved. Relieved that she looked just right. Relieved that I had gotten there in time.

Sandy had always been a beautiful girl, with a perfect, honey-colored complexion, beautiful teeth, and a great smile. And, even in death, she was beautiful.

I don't remember much about Sandy's funeral, except that it hurt more than I could stand. I blocked most of it out of my mind. I still couldn't believe she was gone.

The day after Sandy's funeral was the hardest

day of all. I looked around and saw life going on around me just as it normally does. I wanted the world to stop and notice my pain. But it just kept on spinning, without Sandy.

I felt so alone. I needed my parents, but they were still overseas. By the end of the day, I was all cried out. I did the only thing I could think of: I drove out to Sandy's grave.

Sandy was buried on a gently sloping knoll. A huge shade tree, a barometer for the coming and going seasons, stood anchored beside her. The sun was sinking behind its green leaves.

I sat down beside the freshly mounded dirt. I touched one of the dying flowers—one of hundreds that scented the mound that covered her grave. Without thinking, I started talking to her, as if we were just hanging out as usual.

Only your real friends will tell you when your face is dirty.

SICILIAN PROVERB

"I miss you, Sandy—so much I can't stand it. I can't believe I'm never going to see you again." I had been crying for four days, and yet, new floodgates opened wide, releasing another wave of tears.

"Sandy," I sobbed, "I will always love you. Thank you for being my friend. Thank you for loving me back." I picked up some dirt, squeezing it as though I were squeezing Sandy's hand. I remembered God's promise: "I go to prepare a place for you . . . that where I am, there ye may be also." I had kept my promise. God would keep his to Sandy—and to me. Then I knew: I'd see Sandy again. And I wasn't alone after all.

When a freind is in trouble, don't annoy him by asking if there is anything you can do. Think up something appropriate and do it.

EDGAR WATSON HOWE

I picked a daisy off the grave and headed back to the car. I knew I would never make a promise lightly again. A promise is serious business. A promise never dies.

The Yarn Lady

HOLLY BYRNE

I yanked my bike from the porch rail and took off down the bumpy road. Looking up into the brilliant, blue, summer sky, I shouted my prayer at God.

"Why do my parents treat me like a child?" I yelled. "I'm old enough to babysit my brothers and sisters and do tons of chores, but they won't even let me take a call from a boy! I'm almost fifteen. Please God, make my parents understand."

Better to be a nettle in the side of your friend than his echo.

RALPH WALDO EMERSON

My bike picked up speed as I crested the hill, but I didn't try to slow down. I put my feet on the handlebars and let the bike take over. Tears blurred my vision. Wind blasted around me. I never even heard the car behind me until it zoomed past, narrowly missing me. My bike shimmied out of control and wheeled off the road. I ducked and rolled and landed in a soft, weedy ditch.

"Stupid car!" I yelled, as it drove on. "Don't bother to slow down and check if I'm dead!"

Disgusted, I collapsed back into the weeds and closed my eyes. After a few seconds, I sensed a shadow blocking the sun, I opened my eyes and gasped at the person standing over me. *It's that weird old lady who lives in the run-down trailer! This must be her ditch.* The last thing I wanted to do was deal with her.

"Are you okay?" she asked in a raspy voice.

"I think so." I stood up and brushed grass and dirt off of my jeans. "I better get my bike."

"It's over there, in my flowerbed. I think you flattened some of my peonies."

"I'm sorry," I said, picking up my bike along with a few broken flowers. "They're very pretty."

"Would you like to see something even prettier?" she asked.

"I told my mom I'd be right back," I lied.

"I'm sure she won't mind. I'll show you quickly. Follow me."

Curiosity got the best of me, so I followed the strange old woman. She stopped in front of a small barn, looking as excited as a little kid at Christmas. She pulled the door open, and I peeked inside. I couldn't believe it! Sunshine poured in on a myriad of colors, held like captive rainbows. Sweaters, scarves, hats, mittens,

As iron sharpens iron, so a man sharpens the countenance of his friend.

PROVERBS 27:17

and skeins and skeins of brilliant yarn overflowed from shelves, spilling onto the floor.

"Where did you get all of this?" I asked.

"My brother brings it to me from the knitting mill in the city," she said. "Sometimes there isn't enough yarn left on the skein to start a new article of clothing. And sometimes the knitters just make mistakes. It's all knitting rejects, things they throw away. Can you imagine that?"

Wishing to be friends is quick work, but friendship is slowly ripening fruit.

ARISTOTLE

Noticing her well-worn shoes, I wondered why she didn't try to sell the yarn for money. As she clutched a half-finished sweater to her chest, I shifted my feet and looked back to my bike.

"I really should get going," I said.

A few days later, I slammed the screen door and snatched my bike in another attempt to escape. My parents are so unfair! They hate my friends. Everyone's going to Sarah's party but me. Why don't they trust me? Through my tears, I could see the Yarn Lady's trailer ahead. I thought about pedaling fast with my head down until I had passed her place, but instead, I slowed. I saw her kneeling in a bed of flowers, tossing weeds behind her. She looked up at me with a smile.

"Would you like some iced tea?" she asked.

What was I doing here? Why did I stop? I found myself nodding and following her inside. Her house was a clutter of color—just like the barn! Yarn was stuffed between the cushions of her sofa. It hung like spaghetti out of her kitchen drawers. All that color made the Yarn Lady look extra dull in her shabby clothes.

"Let me move this out of your way," she said, pushing aside a bag of knitting seconds.

"Can't you fix some of these things?" I asked.

"I've tried a few times, but I have trouble," she replied.

In every friend we lose a part of ourselves, and the best part.

ALEXANDER POPE

"I learned how to knit a few years ago in 4-H," I said.

"Do you think you could help me?" she asked.

I wondered what my friends would think of me in this dumpy trailer, teaching this weird old lady how to knit. But since I had nothing better to do, I sat down on her couch. She brought out needles and some yarn. I knitted slowly, showing her where to position the yarn and when to twist the needles. After a few minutes, I gently placed my work in her wrinkled hands. It wasn't long before her wrists were moving in rhythm as she fed yarn to the clicking needles.

Throughout the summer, whenever my troubles overwhelmed me, I felt a pull down the bumpy road toward the Yarn Lady's house. I saw things I never noticed before. Hummingbirds hovered around honeysuckle bushes. Wildflowers sprinkled color around old wooden fence posts. Wheat swayed in waves as the breeze rolled across the fields.

When I visited the Yarn Lady, the wrinkles around her eyes deepened as she showed off her knitted creations. Her joy over her latest batch of yarn seconds was contagious. Once she showed me a skein of raspberry-red yarn with shiny gold strands of thread twisted throughout. It was the most exquisite yarn I had ever seen.

A friend is one who takes me for what I am.

HENRY DAVID THOREAU

One day later that summer, she seemed extra excited when she opened her door to let me in. She proudly modeled her latest knitting project—a transformation from a sleeveless "second" to a beautiful sweater.

"I have something for you," she said with a grin. She handed me a package wrapped in newspaper and tied with red yarn. "Don't open it here, dear. Wait until you get home."

At home I sat on my bed and gently unwrapped the gift. Inside was a beautiful afghan, knitted in a rainbow of colors. To my surprise, in one corner I discovered the raspberry-red yarn with the gold thread running through it.

I showed my mom the afghan and explained my meetings with the Yarn Lady. I worried that she might not approve, but she gave me one of those "mother smiles." The next day, as a thank-you to the Yarn Lady, Mom sent me back to her trailer with some strawberry preserves. In exchange, the Yarn Lady gave me a bag full of mittens for my younger brothers and sisters.

Two are better than one, because they have a good reward for their labor. For if they fall, one will lift up his companion.

ECCLESIASTES 4:9–10

Mom told her friends about the Yarn Lady's yarn. Before long, neighbors began to stop at her house to buy it by the bag full. After school started again, I visited the Yarn Lady less and less. But her yarn business—as well as friendships with the neighbors—kept growing.

After my third year of college, during a visit home, I asked my mother how the Yarn Lady was doing. "I'm sorry, Holly," said Mom. "But she died this past winter."

I ran outside, grabbed my bike, and took off

down the bumpy road to her trailer. Her peonies had spread along the roadside, and tall weeds covered her property. But as I approached the barn, I could see colorful threads poking out from the cracks. Inside, bits and pieces of yarn were scattered all over the floor.

I sat on the steps of the Yarn Lady's vacant trailer with my face buried in my hands. Music drifted down from the trees, interrupting my sorrow. When I looked up—I saw the yarn. Colorful pieces were woven between the mud and twigs in the birds' nests. I smiled through my tears. The Yarn Lady's gift of color and beauty to the world would last for a very long time.

A friend is a present you give yourself.

ROBERT LOUIS STEVENSON

Now, when I feel the urge to flee from my troubles, I often wrap my afghan around my shoulders and look for the gold thread woven in the patch of raspberry-red yarn. Then I thank God for sending me into the ditch that summer day—and for giving me and the Yarn Lady the gift of friendship when we needed it most.

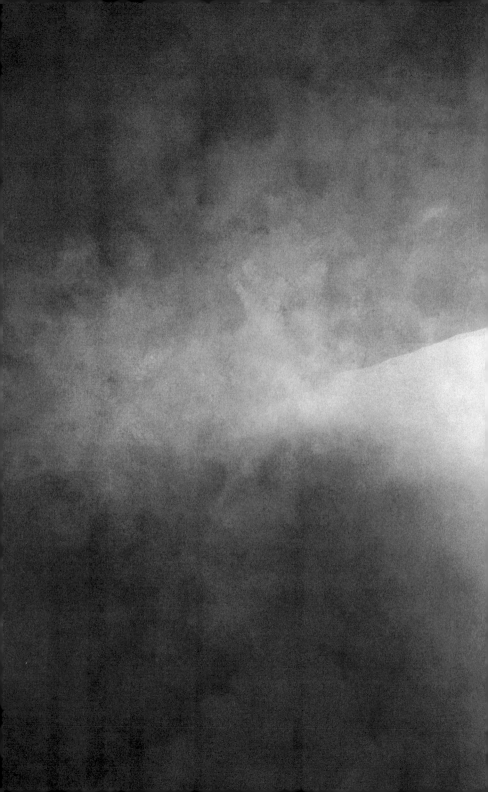

The Power of Love in Action

In Love by the Sea

SAMANTHA FARISON

*I*n August you will fall in love by the sea."

I leaned closer to the newspaper and read my horoscope again. And then I laughed. After all, I was stuck at home for the summer. No sea in sight—and no boyfriend, either.

Suddenly, the phone rang. "Hey, Samantha!" It was my best friend, Ashley. "Guess what! You know how my family's going on vacation to that condo in Crescent Bar in a few weeks? Well, my parents told me I can invite you to come!"

"No way! I'm so there!"

"And the best part is, Brett Olson will be there! Our family goes on vacation with his family almost every year."

Ashley knew that I had a total crush on Brett Olson. He was the most handsome guy in the senior class. He was six feet five inches and a star on the track team. Plus, he had the most incredible brown eyes.

"Ashley, you are the best."

I hung up and immediately

A mirror reflects a man's face, but what he is really like is shown by the kinds of friends he chooses.

PROVERBS 27:19

started making a list of what to take along. Then my horoscope flashed through my mind. *The river at Crescent Bar is sort of like a sea,* I thought. *I'm going to fall in love! With Brett!*

When we arrived at the condo, I found out that Brett and his family wouldn't be coming until several days later. "Bummer!" I told Ashley. "What are we going to do until he gets there?"

She tossed me the suntan lotion. "We can hang out at the pool and get a start on our tans!"

Indeed, we do not really live unless we have friends surrounding us like a firm wall against the winds of the world.

CHARLES HANSON TOWNE

I spent the first day poolside, dreaming of what would happen when Brett got there. I imagined the words we'd say to each other. His big smile. His deep brown eyes. I completely lost sight of the real world.

Until the second day, when I met Joel.

Ashley and I ran into Joel at the pool; we ended up splashing around, eating junk food, and hanging out with him. He was a college freshman, and was staying in Crescent Bar for a few days before heading to Spokane to be a camp counselor. Ashley and I both agreed he was a great guy. The next day, he asked me to go inner-tubing.

I'd never met anyone like Joel. Most of the guys I knew spent a lot of time talking about themselves. But Joel paid attention to me, and he seemed genuinely interested in what I had to say. We had the greatest time inner-tubing. By the end of the day, I realized that I hadn't even thought of Brett once. *Maybe I got my horoscope wrong,* I thought, as we returned our inner-tubes at the rental shack. *Maybe it's Joel that I'm supposed to fall in love with.*

Over the next few days, Joel and I spent a lot of time together. He even pulled out his guitar one afternoon and sang to me. He had written a song for his future wife–whoever she might be—and it was so beautiful.

A faithful friend is an image of God.

FRENCH PROVERB

"So what are you going to do with your life?" he asked me one afternoon, as we sat throwing stones into the river. "What makes you really happy?"

"Me?" No guy had ever asked me questions like that.

"Well . . . I love to paint," I said finally. I told him how I was really into painting furniture, patterning my designs after impressionists like Van Gogh. "Maybe someday I could become a professional artist." I tossed another stone. "How about you?" I asked smiling. "What do you want to be when you grow up?"

"My dream is to become a youth minister," he told me. "God is so important to me. I can't imagine doing anything in life but serving Him."

"That's . . . ummm . . . nice." I really didn't know what to say. Sure, I had gone to church with my family when I was younger. But I didn't know if I even believed in God anymore. *Maybe Joel isn't the guy for me*, I thought.

Joel didn't seem to mind when I finally admitted to him that I was not the religious type. And thankfully, he didn't try to preach to me. We did talk about God for a long

I have learned that to be with those I like is enough.

WALT WHITMAN

time that afternoon. Joel just knew that God was real. He told me that he believed God cares about even the smallest detail of our lives—our dreams as well as our problems. I had never talked about deep subjects like this before.

It was a sad day when Joel packed up his car to leave.

"I'm going to miss you so much," I told him as we hugged good-bye. "Don't forget me."

"I'll never forget you, Samantha."

I choked back tears as he drove off.

I kept to myself the next day and didn't talk much to anyone. As I sat by the pool, I day-dreamed about Joel: his sandy brown hair . . . his melt-you-in-an-instant smile . . . that song he wrote for his future wife . . . *What if it turns out he wrote it for me. . . .*

Stop it, Samantha, I told myself. *That guy is way too religious for you. And Brett's here now.* But hard as I tried, I couldn't stop thinking about Joel. "I'll never forget you, Samantha. . . . "

Brett came over and sat in the lounge chair next to me, interrupting my daydream. "Hi," he said, all friendly-like. "This seat taken?"

Friendship is like money, easier made than kept.

SAMUEL BUTLER

A little flash of Brett-adoration came over me. "All yours!" I said.

"So who's the guy?" Brett asked.

"Umm—a friend I met here," I said. "He's in college." *That probably sounded so stupid,* I thought.

"That's nice," he said. Brett's muscles rippled as he stood up. "Well, I'm going for a swim."

Brett thinks I'm taken! Suddenly, I was more con-fused than ever. *Have I blown it?*

That evening, Joel's car pulled up.

"What are you doing here?" I shouted, running up to meet him.

"I came to see you!"

"You drove two hours, all the way back from Spokane, to see me?"

He reached into his pocket. "I came to give you this."

Is he giving me his phone number? A love note? An engagement ring? My heart sank a little as he handed me a rainbow-colored bracelet with the letters, "W.W.J.D." woven into it.

"Ahhh," I said. I'd seen kids at school with these. "What Would Jesus Do, right?"

"Yeah," Joel said. "Hey—I can't stay. I need to get back. I just wanted you to have the bracelet."

A friend loves at all times, and a brother is born for adversity.
PROVERBS 17:17

He got in his car and started the engine. "You're really a special person."

I put my new bracelet on and waved at Joel as he drove off. Deep down, I knew he wouldn't be back to see me again. But I felt okay about that, somehow. Like our time together had been just right—and long enough.

Back at the condo, Brett was sitting on the steps, listening to his CD. "Hey, what's up?" he nodded.

"Not much." I sat down next to him. "Brett?"

"Yeah?"

"What makes you happy? What do you dream about?"

"Huh?" He looked at me, confused. "Don't tell me you're getting all sappy on us now."

I watched as he ejected a CD and started digging through his case for another. *What did I ever see in this guy?* I thought. *Compared to Joel, he's about as deep as a two-inch puddle.*

To hear complaints with patience, even when complaints are vain, is one of the duties of friendship.

SAMUEL JOHNSON

The rest of the vacation was okay, but it sure didn't turn out the way I'd planned. My dreams of couplehood with Brett had fizzled. And my new dream guy—Joel— was headed off to college and probably seminary and who knows where else. Back home, I dumped my suitcase out on my bed and started to put stuff away. The colorful bracelet Joel gave me caught my eye.

W.W.J.D.?

I looked at the bracelet again.

W.W.J.D.?

That Sunday, I went to church. And I actually enjoyed it. I found myself going back the next week . . . and the next. There was something about being in church that made me feel positive about life—

hopeful and excited about the future. It was that same feeling I had on vacation, when I was talking to Joel about deep things, things that really mattered. As the weeks passed, I began to understand how Joel could be sure that God was real.

In the end, I never did hook up with Brett or Joel. But that W.W.J.D. bracelet became my favorite piece of jewelry. And these days, God is a very real, very important part of my life.

One of the most beautiful qualities of true friendship is to understand and to be understood.

Seneca

I hardly ever read my horoscope anymore, even though in a weird way mine was right that day. I did fall in love by the sea. But it wasn't with Brett— or Joel. I fell in love with God that summer. And it's a love affair I know will last forever.

Only a Dime

PAT EGAN DEXTER

*C*arl was the new guy on the job. He was tall and handsome, with wavy blond hair that flopped onto his forehead and deep-blue eyes that seemed to take in everything. I watched him walk past the cashier's counter where I worked. He smiled at me and I smiled back. Three of us girls had been giggling about him over lunch. We discovered he was single, a part-time worker, and a student, like me. He also lived on the west side of town, as I did. I kept trying to think of ways to get him to notice me.

> *Friendship is the golden thread that ties the hearts of all the world.*
>
> JOHN EVELYN

We worked in a busy drugstore in downtown Chicago. This particular day was an especially rushed one, so there was little opportunity for me to talk to Carl during working hours. I tried to think of some excuse to talk with him later, but I couldn't. I wondered if he was interested in me too. He looked over my way a lot; and when our eyes met, he smiled. I could watch him as he arranged items on the shelves, because much of my work was automatic.

The cash register was one of those that dispenses the correct change at the push of a button. But it was the responsibility of the cashier to see that all the coin slots were full. This day, in my distracted state of mind, I had filled the dime dispensers unevenly, and one dime slot was empty before the other. I didn't notice it at first. By the time it occurred to me what had happened, I had cheated a few customers out of part of their change. But not one customer had mentioned it. In fact, very few people had even counted their change.

At the end of the workday I looked around for Carl, but I didn't see him. I balanced my cash register receipts against the money and found that I was sixty cents over. Yes, I told myself, that would be just about the number of dimes that people were shorted.

> *If, instead of a gem or even a flower, we would cast the gift of a lovely thought into the heart of a friend, that would be giving as angels give.*
>
> GEORGE MACDONALD

I hesitated a few minutes and then decided to keep the overage and not mention this to anyone. After all, it was only sixty cents, a dime here and a dime there, and no one was going to miss one little dime.

The next day at the register I filled my coin slots full, as the manager had instructed. After a while when the dime slots became empty, I decided to fill only one of them—just to see if anyone would notice, I told myself.

For the next hour, customers came and went. But no one noticed when his change was short ten cents.

No one, that is, except handsome Carl.

"Hey, Patti," he said, "one of your dime slots is empty."

"Oh," I said, smiling. "I guess it is."

I reached into my drawer for another roll of dimes. Carl walked away. I watched him go, then put the roll of dimes back into the drawer.

The best mirror is an old friend.

GEORGE HERBERT

When I checked out that evening, I had profited by over three dollars—enough to pay for my lunch. And not one person had complained.

I told myself that what I was doing wasn't really stealing. No one even noticed. I already had it worked out in my mind that if someone did complain, I would simply act surprised and say, "Oh, one dime slot is empty." Then I would give that customer the shorted dime. After all, I rationalized, I did need the money. And I reasoned that I wasn't hurting anyone. The people who didn't even count their change must not have needed it. After I finished checking out, I looked around the store for Carl. But again he was gone.

The next day, almost from the beginning of my shift, I left one dime slot empty. Customers came and customers went, and only once did someone say, "Miss, my change is incorrect." Then I quickly fixed my mistake.

Later in the day, Carl walked by. "How are you doing today?" he asked.

Our friendship brings sunshine to the shade, and shade to the sunshine.

THOMAS BURKE

"Fine." I smiled at him. I wondered if he was going to ask me out. If he didn't, and since he had approached me, I considered asking him if he'd like to go out for a Coke or something after work.

"Your dime slot is empty again," he said.

"Oh," I said. I reached into the drawer for a roll of dimes. "I was wondering," I began, "if—"

He interrupted me. "There are many ways to steal," Carl said. "And setting up a coin changer incorrectly is one of them."

I could feel my face flush, so I looked away. I had thought he liked me. But now his voice had a stern, almost mean, tone to it. And I hated hearing what he was saying.

"Maybe we can fool the customers," he said. "And maybe we can even fool the manager. But we can never fool ourselves. I don't know about you, Patti, but I was taught the Ten Commandments. And I don't think it would be worth a dime, or any amount of money, to feel the way I would feel after breaking one of God's laws."

Then Carl walked away. I was so embarrassed I wanted to hide. But there was no place to go. So I busied myself with my work and tried not to look in Carl's direction.

The only way to have a friend is to be one.

RALPH WALDO EMERSON

Suddenly I was very angry with him. *What business is it of his what I do?* I thought. *He isn't the manager. The guy is just a Goody Two-shoes.* I took the roll of dimes and filled the money changer. But I couldn't stop thinking about what Carl had said. He wasn't the only one who'd been brought up on the Ten Commandments.

And then it hit me. I'd fooled myself into thinking I wasn't stealing. But I was.

I had wanted Carl to notice me, but he didn't smile at me or even look my way the rest of that day.

I wondered if he would tell the manager. I even considered quitting my job.

At the end of the workday I turned in my overage. Carl must not have said anything, because the manager was surprised.

"One of my dime slots was empty," I said. "I'll be more careful from now on."

The manager nodded but said nothing.

When I left the building, Carl was just ahead of me. He was heading toward the steps to the elevated train on the busy downtown street.

His jaw was set and his back was stiff, and he was hurrying. *Probably to avoid me*, I thought. I slowed. He didn't have to worry about my trying to catch up with him. I dreaded seeing him then, the next day, or ever again.

A friend may well be reckoned the masterpiece of nature.
RALPH WALDO EMERSON

I bit my lip. Suddenly a great sadness came over me. He wasn't a Goody Two-shoes. He was right, and I had been wrong. I should have known better. Maybe the extra money was nice, but the stealing wasn't worth it. Silently I asked God to forgive me for what I had done.

Carl had done me a favor. Something inside me told me that I should tell Carl that and thank him. I knew if I did, it would be easier for us to work together.

I ran after him and caught up with him just as he reached the stairway to the elevated station. "Carl," I said, tapping him on the shoulder. "I was wrong. Thanks for setting me straight."

He seemed surprised at my words. He leaned against the railing and stared directly at me. Again I was embarrassed. It hadn't been easy for me to say that. He could have at least said, "Okay."

I could hear the elevated train begin to pull away from the station. Finally I shrugged and started up the stairs. Even though it didn't seem to matter to Carl that I had admitted my wrongdoing, I was glad I had done it. At least I knew that God forgave me.

Halfway up the stairs, I felt a tap on my shoulder. I turned to see Carl. He was smiling. "Want to go for a Coke?" he asked over the roar of the train.

> *As long as we love, we serve; as long as we are loved by others, I would almost say that we are indispensable; and no man is useless while he has a friend.*
>
> ROBERT LOUIS STEVENSON

Just Another Day

MIDDY RANDERSON

his is just another day, I told myself on February 14 as I looked around the bookstore where I worked. The shelves overflowed with heart-shaped gifts, valentine cards, and bright-red books with "I Love You" on the cover. But I wasn't feeling very loved. My longtime boyfriend had recently left me for someone else. My parents were far away, working overseas. No one would be sending me a valentine.

Without friends, no one would choose to live, though he had all other goods.

ARISTOTLE

Putting on a friendly face, I made small talk with the customers. I helped one frantic guy choose a teddy bear for his best girlfriend, and a chocolate rose for someone he called his "best-friend girl." One young woman spent nearly an hour picking the right card. "I think he's going to propose tonight," she gushed. I forced a smile and counted the minutes until closing.

As I was about to lock up, a white-hared woman came in. She wasn't a regular customer, but her face seemed familiar. *Have I seen her browsing here before?* I wondered. She walked up to me, smiling broadly, and held out her hand. I looked down at a tiny, heart-shaped pincushion covered with delicate red fabric and lace. "I made this for you," she said.

I didn't know what to say. I took the gift, cupping it in my hands, stroking the soft fabric and admiring the fineness of her craft.

"I'm a widow," the woman said. "Most of my friends have died, but I still sew these valentines every year." She turned to look at me on her way out. "There's plenty of love in this world," she said. "I believe we should share it."

I never saw her again, but when Christmastime rolled around (yet another holiday when I got the blues) I remembered her example. I packed inexpensive makeup bags with a comb, toothpaste, mirror, scented soap, and perfume samples, and wrapped them in bright paper as gifts for the women at a local shelter—women who are often forgotten even if their children are given presents. A holiday is just another day after all—another day when we can fulfill Christ's commandment to love one another.

Friends share all things.
PYTHAGORAS

Here's a Tip—Don't Mess with Hilda

SHANNON VAN ROEKEL

"Shannon, your order's up! We don't pay you to loiter!"

Karen passed me in the aisle, rolling her eyes and smiling sympathetically. I needed all the sympathy I could get.

This was my second day working at the restaurant as a waitress. I was only fifteen, so I had been lucky to land this job in the first

Fate chooses our relatives, we choose our friends.

JACQUES DELILLE

place. My older sister, who'd been working there for a year already, had given me a good referral to the bosses—only after threatening to delimb my body if I didn't do a good job. I had promised her that I would do the very best I possibly could. And now I was well on my way to being fired, all because of one person: Hilda, the manager.

Her very name struck fear in the hearts of the entire staff. Not since Queen Mary ruled England and earned herself the title "Bloody Mary" had a female held reign with so much terror. Or so it seemed.

Hilda watched me like a hawk. If I didn't have all

the tables in my section wiped down and set up perfectly, she yelled. If one of my customers ran out of coffee, she yelled. When I filled out an order she would check it for mistakes—and yell. At the end of the first day I went home in tears. Today didn't look any better.

"Excuse me please, miss, could you take our order? We're in quite a hurry." The man was waiting at a table with his wife and two small children.

"Um . . . yes, sir, what can I get for you?" Maybe their order would be quick. I glanced over at the food waiting to be picked up at the pass bar.

"I'd like the breakfast special, please," the wife ordered.

A friend is a person with whom I may be sincere. Before him, I may think aloud.

RALPH WALDO
EMERSON

"Why not make that two?" Her husband smiled up at me, and I silently blessed him for his quick decision-making skills.

"And for the children?" I asked sweetly.

"Carly and Mikey, what would you like? The waffles with strawberries and whipped cream look lovely, mmmmmmmm . . . ."

"I hate whipped cream," declared Mikey.

"I want french fries," said Carly.

"Okay, a side of fries, two specials, and . . . " I looked at Mikey hopefully.

"Oh no!" the mother said, glaring at me. "Carly certainly may not have french fries for breakfast."

As she gently and patiently proceeded to explain the basic elements of nutrition to her little darlings, I wanted to scream with frustration.

When I finally got back to the pass bar, I knew my life was over.

There stood Hilda with her hands on her hips.

"So, you decided to come and deliver your order, did you?"

"Sorry, but that table took for- ever—" I started to explain, but Hilda cut me off—big time. I don't remember the names she called me or exactly what she said, but it hurt. No one had ever talked to me that way.

There is nothing on this earth more to be prized than true friendship.

THOMAS AQUINAS

The rest of the day passed in a total blur. It was like a nightmare I couldn't wake up from.

I cried the whole way home.

There was small comfort in the twenty dollars in tips jingling in my apron pocket. They hadn't fired me yet, but I knew I couldn't work there anymore. Obviously I wasn't cut out to be a waitress. And I would never go back to face that terrible woman. She hated me. She looked at me with disgust, like I was a germ or something. She'd hurt me deliberately and cruelly. I could take some criticism, but this was way over the limit.

Love your enemies.

Where had that thought come from?

"Oh no, Lord, You wouldn't say that if You'd seen what she did to me today." No sooner were the words out of my mouth than I remembered He had seen everything.

Whoever slaps you on your right cheek, turn to him the other also.

Whoever shall force you to go one mile, go with him two.

I was shaking my head. Maybe I should forgive Hilda for her behavior, but I couldn't go back there and face more of the same.

Your wealth is where your friends are.

PLAUTUS

Bless those who persecute you. I choked. Bless her? "The greatest blessing I could give Hilda would be my resignation. Right, God?"

Silence.

It would be so embarrassing to go back.

"Lord, I'll go if I have to, but You need to change my heart. And Lord, how can I bless her?"

Flowers.

And so I found myself standing in the florist's, looking at arrangements of all kinds. I finally settled on a bouquet of twelve long-stemmed pink roses. The Lord had even provided me with the exact amount I needed to buy them: twenty dollars.

I went back to the restaurant and sneaked in the kitchen door, flowers behind my back, hoping she'd be in the office.

"What are you doing back here?" Hilda barked when I knocked on her open door. "Haven't you had enough for one day?" She looked tired and her eyes had dark smudges under them. Her face was etched with sad, thin lines that pulled her mouth down and gave her a pained look. I wondered fleetingly what could have happened to make her life so hard.

Real friendship is shown in times of trouble; prosperity is full of friends.

EURIPIDES

"I just want to say I'm sorry for giving you so much stress today. I hope we have a better day tomorrow." Amazingly, I meant every word I was saying. I held out the flowers.

"You went and got those for me?" Disbelief filled her voice. "I can't remember the last time someone gave me flowers." Tears squeezed out of her eyes and her chin crumpled. "Shannie, can we start over?"

And then an amazing thing happened. We were hugging and laughing. A friendship had begun.

All because of a blessing.

Born in a Stable

JOSEPH BALES

That Christmas Eve my brothers, my mom and I were coming back from my aunt's house. It was a long drive home, and everyone was tired and a little discouraged. My aunt's tree had so many presents under it, and there was nothing under ours. My father had walked out on us more than four months earlier and had only paid one month of child support. Mom was working three jobs; none of them paid well.

The real friend is he or she who can share all our sorrow and double our joys.

B. C. FORBES

I had made my mom a small present at school that I knew she'd like. I also knew it wouldn't take the weariness from her eyes or the exhaustion from her body. She cried a lot now and hardly ever smiled. Neither my two older brothers nor I could help by getting jobs. My oldest brother, James, was only twelve, John was nine, and I was seven. We did the chores on the farm and what we could around the house. That was it.

As we pulled into the driveway, Mom reminded me it was my night to do chores. We had chickens, ducks, sheep, and a cow. We had to sell many of our animals because we didn't have enough money to feed them. Our dad had taken our dog and sold it. For twenty-five dollars. One of our cats had gotten run over, and we could not afford to take it to the vet. We prayed a lot, but we struggled too. Every day there was something else to deal with.

I headed toward the shed. I had to gather eggs, make sure the chickens were all locked in, and open the gate to let the sheep into the pasture. First I let the sheep out and then I checked the chicken pen. Something was wrong. The door was already shut. I looked in. No chickens!

If you make friends with yourself, you will never be alone.
MAXWELL MALTZ

"Mom! John! James!" I yelled. "The chicken door is shut and all the chickens are roosting everywhere. I need help getting them in."

We would have to gather up all the chickens. Meanwhile the sheep had to be kept back or they would go into the chicken pen and eat the grain. There were thirty chickens out in trees or on fences, and any one of them could have become a raccoon's Christmas dinner.

I got a flashlight and went looking for the stray chickens. Some of them had gone into the sheep's pen. I searched with the light and saw a huge lump in one corner. As I walked closer I realized it was a ewe. She did not get up as I came closer. I could see her roll on her side and give a push. Moving the flashlight down I saw a nose and one leg protruding out of her. She was in labor and the lamb was stuck, either because it was too big or in the wrong position.

"There's a ewe out here in labor," I called. "Quick, help me get her into the shed so I can see. She's having problems."

I put down my flashlight and ran to her, grabbed her around the neck as she started struggling and began pulling her to the nearest shed that had electricity.

Every man should have a fair-sized cemetery in which to bury the faults of his friends.

HENRY BROOKS ADAMS

James helped me, and we finally got her inside. Mom went to get towels ready. Then Mom held the ewe's head while James tried to push the baby back so it would be in a better position. He got it partly in but couldn't continue. His hands were too big because she was not fully dilated.

"Joseph," she said, "see what you can feel."

I traded places with James and reached my hand in. I felt the lamb's head and traced my hand down the neck. I felt one leg. It was in the right position. I traced back up the head and down the other side. I felt another leg. It was folded back. Once I got hold of the leg, I straightened it so both were forward with the nose. As my hand was feeling the lamb, the ewe had a contraction. I felt her body tighten on my arm, and then the contraction passed.

"I think I got it," I said. I pulled my arm out of the ewe. Only minutes later, with her next push, the lamb's nose and two hooves showed. The ewe was so tired she did not have the energy to push again. James gently pulled on the legs to help guide the lamb out. The ewe tried again and could not push the lamb out completely. James pulled again and out came the lamb. Mom wiped the birthing bag from his face. He was not breathing. I blew into his nose and he sneezed. He was alive!

Friendship without self-interest is one of the rare and beautiful things of life.
JAMES FRANCIS BYRNES

Mom finished cleaning its face, then picked up the lamb and laid it by the ewe's nose. She looked at us, smelled her lamb, and started licking him clean.

"No wonder she had problems," John said. "He's huge. I wonder how long she was in labor."

"Who knows?" James said. "But it's way past midnight. Merry Christmas!"

I looked around at my family. My mom was smiling again. James had his arm draped around John's shoulder. The baby lamb was struggling to stand already. Everything seemed all right.

"A long time ago on this morning," I said, "Jesus was born. Angels were singing and all the farm animals were gathered around looking at his birth. I'll bet there were ewes and lambs in the stable with him."

My mom started crying, but she said they were happy tears. We all hugged, and smiles were on everyone's faces. I went out and got fresh hay, straw, and water for the ewe and baby. John and James made sure the lamb received its mother's first milk by getting it to nurse. Mom just kept crying and smiling at us through it all.

Actions, not words, are the true criterion of the attachment of friends.

GEORGE WASHINGTON

We all went into the house. The tree still did not have very many presents under it, yet it looked different. We had already received a wonderful present out in the shed. We had all been part of the miracle of birth. I could imagine that ewe and her lamb at the stable with Jesus long ago. And I knew he was with us that night, and through all our struggles. It was a great Christmas after all.

Me and Mrs. Baretta

HELEN FRANCES WEST

I sighed loudly and flopped down on my hospital bed and looked out my window at the snow, which was cascading down on the empty parking lot. The only thing moving outside were snowplows. *My friends are probably having a great time on the slopes*, I thought.

Three days ago, I'd been packing for the junior class ski trip to Killington, Vermont, when the sharp pain in my side hit. Mom rushed me to the doctor and, after a thorough exam, he gave me the news.

"Well, it's not your appendix. But I'm not sure what's wrong. If there is a cyst or an ovary causing you trouble in there, we'll have to remove it," he said, snapping my file shut.

> *There is one thing better than making a new friend, and that is keeping an old one.*
>
> ELMER G. LETERMAN

Now, I found myself in this green room, hooked up to an IV, with no release date in sight. After running tests, my doctor still didn't know what was wrong, so he had decided to operate. But the weather had other ideas. A blizzard shut down all the roads, and half of the hospital staff couldn't make it to work. My parents couldn't even get out of our driveway to visit me! My big entertainment was listening to the old lady in the next bed cough and wheeze.

God, why did this have to happen to me? And why couldn't I be in a room with another teenage girl? I wondered how long it would be before I could go back to being a cheerleader again.

I glanced over at the old lady. *Lily Baretta,* the chart above her read. She looked about ninety, all shriveled and pale. It was hard to tell what was wrong with her. Her face was covered in gross purple welts.

Mrs. Baretta's phone rang. She just sat there and stared straight ahead. *Why doesn't she answer it?*

One is taught by experience to put a premium on those few people who can appreciate you for what you are.
GAIL GODWIN

That afternoon, during visiting hours, her daughter arrived, snow melting off her boots. Mrs. Baretta was asleep. "My mother was a Gold Star mother, you know," she said, patting Mrs. Baretta's hand.

"What's that?" I said.

"She lost a son in the Second World War. My older brother, Mario. Her only son."

"Oh, sorry." I wasn't sure what to say.

After about an hour, Mrs. Baretta's daughter put her coat back on. "I need to get going," she told me. "I walked all the way from the other side of town. The snow's so bad, even buses aren't getting through."

I turned my head on the pillow to look at Mrs. Baretta after her daughter left. A Gold Star mother. She must be one of those old ladies who ride in parades, in cars with a star pasted on them. I tried to imagine her waving to a crowd. She was awake, but she was gazing straight ahead, as usual. It was pretty obvious that she wasn't strong enough to wave to anybody now.

Some people come into our lives and quickly go. Some stay for a while and leave footprints on our hearts. And we are never, ever the same.

Author Unknown

Luckily, whatever was wrong with me didn't affect my appetite. I guzzled down dinner—a chilled pear half on a wilted slice of iceberg lettuce, chicken pot pie, carrots, and applesauce. I even ate the Jell-O.

Then I looked over at Mrs. Baretta's tray. On her plate sat a single slice of white bread. *You've got to be kidding*, I thought. *That can't be all they're giving her!*

The next morning, I launched into the woman

who dropped off the menu. "How come you only brought this lady a piece of bread for dinner?"

"That's all that was checked on her menu."

"She obviously can't see well enough to read it, much less check off what she wants!"

"Well, we're pretty shorthanded around here," she said. "I'll see what I can do." She turned and left.

If I cannot do great things, I can do small things in a great way.

JAMES FREEMAN
CLARKE

Now I was getting mad. *She expects me to fill it out!* I thought. *I'm a patient here, not a nurse. I* switched the TV channel.

A few minutes later, Mrs. Baretta's phone rang, and rang.

All right, already. I got out of bed, picked up the receiver, and held it to her ear. Mrs. Baretta's daughter's voice came through the phone. "Hi, Mother . . . it's a beautiful blue sky today. . . . "

Mrs. Baretta was still staring straight ahead, but she was smiling a little. *She's stuck here, too,* I thought. *And she's not complaining. Maybe I should help her out a little.*

That afternoon, I stood at the end of Mrs. Baretta's bed and bellowed out the menu selections. "Chicken noodle soup or beef vegetable?"

She smiled.

"Nod if you want chicken noodle soup."

She nodded.

We went through the entire menu, from appetizer to beverages.

For the next couple of days, we had our own little routine. I'd fill out her menu for her, then do mine. When the meals came, I ate mine quickly, then went over to help her. It took me a few tries to get the fork into her shaky hand and then up to her mouth. I held the cup so she could sip her tea. Pretty soon I got used to looking at those gross purple welts on her face. Helping her actually started to make me feel better.

On my fifth night in the hospital, I woke from a sound sleep and looked at the red digits on the clock next to me: 2:00. Mrs. Baretta's buzzer light was on. *The nurse will come soon*, I thought, rolling over. My eyes opened again at 2:10. Her buzzer was still on. I sat up. Something's wrong. Mrs. Baretta's thin hand was still pressing the buzzer.

I leapt out of bed and walked barefoot into

> *You give but little when you give of your possessions. It is when you give of yourself that you truly give.*
>
> KAHLIL GIBRAIN

the hall, rolling my IV pole along with me. "Nurse!" I yelled. The halls were empty. "Nurse!" I yelled louder, venturing further down the hall.

"What are you doing?" A nurse finally rounded the corner.

"Mrs. Baretta needs help!"

"Honey, I know, but we're understaffed. . . . "

"Nobody's answering her buzzer."

With a *hurrumfph*, the nurse headed into our room and changed Mrs. Baretta's bedpan. "Now get back to bed!" she barked.

The next time Mrs. Baretta pushed her buzzer, I buzzed, too, pressing my call button hard until a nurse entered our room.

Kindness is love in work clothes.
AUTHOR UNKNOWN

Two days later, I finally had my surgery. "It turned out to be a bad infection," the doctor told me in the recovery room. "Two weeks of antibiotics will take care of it. You'll be back cheerleading in no time!"

I sure hoped he was right. A week after leaving the hospital, I was in my room practicing a routine for an upcoming basketball game when the phone rang.

I heard Mom answer the phone in the other room, then she appeared in the doorway. "That was Mrs. Baretta's daughter," she said. "You know, the daughter of that woman who was your roommate at the hospital?"

"Uh-huh . . . "

"Mrs. Baretta died this morning."

Now I think I understand why Mrs. Baretta and I ended up being roommates. She needed help, and I needed to help somebody. Turns out God was smiling down on me all along. Me—and Mrs. Baretta.

The great use of life is to spend it for something that outlasts it.

WILLIAM JAMES

Blue Sky

Tara Karr

Blue sky, birds singing, soft breeze—a sterotypically gorgeous morning. I sit curled up with my pillow and Bible, trying hard to focus on the beauty of the day. No matter how pristine the landscape, there is nothing that can take away the fact that nine little campers are fast asleep in the cabin behind me, poised to wake up, throw up, or throw something and disturb my peace.

The best things are nearest: breath in your nostrils, light in your eyes, flowers at your feet, duties at your hand, the path of God just before you.

ROBERT LOUIS STEVENSON

When I move to the nearly empty dining hall for staff devotions, the possibilities aren't much different—in fact they're a little worse. Those nine sleepers could now be wide awake, breaking bunks and brooms, or even more treacherously not awake and quickly running out of time to take a shower before breakfast. Although I hope and pray for squeaky clean campers and cabin when I return at 8:15, I know there will still be someone's wet towel on my bunk and someone else who's curled up in the bottom of her sleeping bag and refusing to get up for anything less than a hurricane.

We progress through the day with a few struggles—three Bibles are lost in piles of clothes just before morning devotions, and everyone remembers to use the restroom before chapel except the girl sitting on the far end, away from the aisle. One camper's creative hairstyle has to be cut out by the nurse, two girls set their eyes on the boys who haven't changed clothes since the week started, and a few more collect all the bunk bed mattresses and make a fort in front of our cabin door. The sisters who just had to be together are fighting, and two of a trio of best friends are leaving the third in the dust. My Band-Aids, gum, and hair ties disappear from my duffle bag pocket at the slightest hint of being willing to share. When I take a little break to say "hi" to a friend on beach duty, I'm begged by nine soggy girls to go swimming in a lake with a name meaning "green water"—and I can barely dog paddle.

> *God does not so much need people to do extraordinary things as he needs people who do ordinary things extraordinarily well.*
>
> WILLIAM BARCLAY

Whatever comes, let us be content withal. Among God's blessings there is no one small.

ROBERT HERRICK

When we're chosen last for dinner, I am met with whines regardless of the fact that we went first for lunch. At evening chapel, we sing my favorite song, but the girls claim to be too hot and tired to do the motions, and watch like I'm nuts. When we finally get ready for bed, someone throws her retainer away (again) and I forget my toothpaste and have to borrow some from another cabin leader, who points out that one of my campers forgot her sunscreen before swim time and now resembles a boiled lobster.

After scrambling into bed, still in my jeans, when the lights-out bell rings, I lie on my cot and listen to creaky wooden bunk beds, rustling late night snack wrappers, and whispers that are slightly less audible than whoever is snoring.

I say my prayers and thank God for another unbelievable day in the world's best summer job for me—service for my Savior at Cocolalla Lake Bible Camp. The weight of the struggles that seemed as landmarks in my day are nothing compared to the value of the nine girls sleeping (or maybe not sleeping yet) in the bunks around me. God allows me to

look past the chaos, confusion, and incessant inter-
ruptions, and remember the camper who voluntarily
read her Bible for the first time that morning, the
other who is struggling with a back-
ground of drugs, the one who is
nervous about making friends, the
girl who accepted Jesus into her
heart that very night on the cabin's
front porch—and even more.

I fall asleep filled with a peace
infinitely better than having one
silent moment on a picturesque
morning, and can't wait to wake up to another complicated, beautiful day.

*Contentment is
not the fulfillment
of what you want,
but the realization
of how much you
already have.*

AUTHOR UNKNOWN

Stranger at Table #5

CORYNE WONG-COLLINGSWORTH

I t was five days before Christmas and the café where I worked in northern California glowed with strands of red and green chili peppers. Holiday music played over the sound system, and my co-workers excitedly discussed their plans. "Doing aything special?" they asked me. I shook my head.

I was three thousand miles from my family in Hawaii, pursuing my lifelong dream of becoming a pediatric nurse. I attended classes all day, then went straight to my full-time waitress job at night. After months of this hectic schedule, I was totally exhausted— and extremely homesick.

> *Love is my decision to make your problem my problem.*
>
> ROBERT HAROLD SCHULLER

I had always looked forward to the holidays. But this December I felt unable to go on. In my prayers I told God that if I could just get home to see my mom, dad, and brothers, I could survive the next two years until I graduated. But how? Rent, tuition, textbooks, and other expenses left me with no extra cash. Money to go home? I barely had money to buy food to eat!

"I'm on my break. Cover for me, will you?" asked Maribelle, another waitress, as she passed me on her way to the employees' lounge. "By the way, there's this guy at table five," she said. "He's been sitting there for more than an hour, not making any trouble but not ordering anything either."

She paused. "It's like he's waiting for somebody."

I looked in the corner. Sure enough, a slim, pleasant-looking man dressed in worn jeans, a red-and-black plaid shirt, and a black baseball cap was just sitting. Alone. I went over, trying to muster a smile. "I'm Cory," I said to him. "Please let me know if you want anything."

I was turning to walk away when the man spoke. He had a soft, low voice, but somehow I could hear it clear and plain in the noisy restaurant. "I'd like an order of nachos," he said. "And a glass of water."

My heart sank. The nachos were the cheapest thing on the menu, which meant that I wouldn't get much of a tip. I figured maybe this guy was broke, and I sure

> *If we have got the true love of God shed abroad in our hearts, we will show it in our lives. We will not have to go up and down the earth proclaiming it. We will show it in everything we say or do.*
>
> DWIGHT LYMAN MOODY

knew how that felt, so I tried my best to make him feel okay. "Coming right up," I said.

I returned a few minutes later and slid the nachos in front of him. "That will be two dollars and ninety-five cents," I said.

He reached into his pocket and handed me a single bill. "Keep the change," he said softly.

Give what you have. To someone it may be better than you dare to think.

HENRY WADSWORTH LONGFELLOW

I looked at it—then looked again. "Excuse me, sir," I said. "This is a hundred-dollar bill."

"I know," he replied softly.

My eyes opened wide. "I don't understand," I said. "What do you want from me?"

"Not a thing," he said, looking straight into my eyes. He stood up. "Call your mother tonight," he said. "Merry Christmas." Then he moved in the direction of the front door. When I turned to thank him, he was nowhere is sight, although the exit was at least fifty feet away.

The rest of the evening passed in a blur. I finished work, went back to my apartment, and put the money on the table. I had just turned on the television when the phone rang. It was my mother. She told me that my brothers had bought an airline ticket to get me home for Christmas. But they could only afford the fare one way. "Can you possibly manage the return fare?" she asked.

At that moment a commercial flashed on television. A major airline was announcing cut-rate fares to Hawaii—one way for ninety-nine dollars. I jumped off the sofa, shouting, "Thank you, God! I'm going home!"

I returned to my studies filled with new spirit and determination, and today I'm a registered nurse. I'll never forget the mysterious stranger who helped me in my time of need. He appeared with no halo or sparkling wings, but he was a sort of angel just the same.

We are never more like God than when we give.

CHARLES SWINDOLL

Crash on Highway 20

BY GARY WILLING

I threw my duffel bag into my truck and started off on the 200-mile drive from my apartment in Marietta, Georgia, to my family's South Carolina home. I was looking forward to relaxing, spending a few days thinking about where my life was headed.

Love has power to give in a moment what toil can scarcely reach in an age.

JOHANN WOLFGANG VON GOETHE

Lately I had been wondering what I'd accomplished, what I really had to offer. It wasn't easy waiting tables to pay the rent so I could pursue my passion for music. I played bass guitar in a band. We had landed a regular gig, but I still couldn't quit my day job. "Just follow your heart," my schoolteacher mom had always told me, but I wondered if that was enough. I wanted to contribute something, to make a difference. How would I know if I was on the right path?

When I left that morning, the sky was full of clouds and the air was nippy. I was glad I had ditched my usual sandals in favor of thick, new socks and hiking boots. After merging onto I-20, I pushed back my baseball cap and set the cruise con-trol, humming along with the radio. At least the long drive would give me some time to try to sort out the answers to my questions. There were few other cars, and the road was long and welcoming. I could feel the tension seep out of me.

I was making good time, and halfway through my journey it looked as if I'd be able to make it to an early lunch with my family. I approached a hill and accelerated. As I reached the crest, I saw brake lights ahead and hit my own brake pedal hard. A bus had stopped. A car, too. Oh, great! A delay, I thought. Then I spotted an overturned van on the highway and saw injured people lying all over the road. I reached for my cell phone—my eyes riveted to the scene—and dialed 911.

> *Loving, like prayer, is a power as well as a process. It's curative. It is creative.*
> ZONA GALE

"Send help quick," I said to the woman who answered. "There's been a terrible accident."

"Where is it?" the dispatcher asked.

"Uh . . . I don't know," I said, feeling utterly useless. "Somewhere on I-20. Please hurry."

"Sir, drive down to the next mile marker and tell me the number so we can locate the accident."

"Okay, I'll try, ma'am," I said. I pulled onto the

shoulder and sped alongside the road, searching for the tiny green sign. "I see it!" I almost shouted into the phone. "It's 146."

Help is on the way, I told myself. *Now what?* I had watched countless rescue shows on television about heroes who had helped people out of disastrous situations. But I had no first-aid skills, nothing to offer the accident victims.

Mom . . . she always knows the right thing to do. I picked up the phone again and called her. "I just passed a horrible accident on the road. I called 911. I don't know what I should do now," I poured out.

"Gary, go back. Maybe you can help someone," Mom said.

She was right. I at least had to try to do something. My heart hammering, I exited and got back on the road going the opposite direction. I was in uncharted territory—what did I know about this sort of situation? God, please, use me somehow to help someone, I prayed.

By the time I got back to the accident scene, a

What does love look like? It has hands to help others. It has feet to hasten to the poor and needy. It has eyes to see misery and want. It has ears to hear the sighs and sorrows of men. That is what love looks like.

SAINT AUGUSTINE OF HIPPO

few other drivers had stopped to help. I got out. The air smelled of radiator fluid and it was eerily quiet—except for the moans of the injured.

Two guys in military fatigues were administering IVs to the most critically hurt. Some people were getting blankets out of a car, and I rushed over to give them a hand. My arms were filled with pillows and blankets, but I hesitated before turning to face the victims. Why am I here? Can anything I do really make a difference to these poor people?

The weaker we feel, the harder we lean on God. And the harder we lean, the stronger we grow.
JONI EARECKSON TADA

I started moving among the injured. They were mostly young women. I draped blankets over them, barely able to look at their bruised, bleeding faces. I questioned the ones who were conscious and slowly pieced together what had happened.

They were cheerleaders from the State University of West Georgia, on their way to a camp in Myrtle Beach, South Carolina. When a tire blew out, their van flipped over several times. All thirteen passengers had been thrown from the vehicle.

A dark-haired girl was sprawled on her stomach, right over the highway center line. I knelt beside her. "Where are you hurt?" I asked, covering her with blankets.

"My back," she managed to say.

"Help is coming," I assured her. I started to get up, glancing at the wreckage strewn around me.

Goodness is love in action, love with its hand to the plow, love with the burden on its back, love following his footsteps who went about continually doing good.

JAMES HAMILTON

"Please don't leave me," she said. So I stretched out on that cold pavement right next to her. I lay on my side so we were face to face— and so she couldn't see how badly her friends were hurt.

She tried to push herself up. A warning bell went off in my mind. I remembered reading somewhere that someone seriously injured shouldn't be moved because that could aggravate the injuries. "No, no, lie still," I said.

"But I've got to get off the road," she said. "I'll get run over." She tried again to get up.

"The road's been blocked," I said. "You're safe." She looked confused. I had to get her mind on something else. "What's your name?" I asked.

"Haley," she said. "Haley Black."

"Where are you from?"

"Gainesville, Georgia," she murmured, closing

her eyes. I knew from all those rescue shows that I shouldn't let her fall asleep.

"Haley, Haley, wake up," I said, reaching out to squeeze her hand. Her eyelids flickered open, then closed. *Oh, God, what do I do?* I thought. Suddenly I thought of Haley's parents. She probably wished they were here. They would want to know what had happened. I was debating whether to go back to my truck to get my phone when I spotted a guy nearby with one in his pocket. I borrowed it, then returned to Haley, whose eyes were still closed. "Haley," I said loudly, "would you like me to call your parents for you?"

She blinked a couple of times, then mumbled a phone number. I dialed it and broke the news of the accident to Haley's parents. I told them she was awake and talking and that I would stay with her until an ambulance came.

"Please let us know where they take her," her father said, his voice shaking. "And tell her we'll be with her soon." Then he hung up.

"Your parents are on their way."

"My back really hurts," she said.

"Haley," I said, "I know this might not make sense, but that's a good sign—the fact that you can feel the pain." That seemed to reassure

> *True charity is the desire to be useful to others without thought of recompense.*
>
> EMANUEL SWEDENBORG

her. I picked some shards of glass out of her hair and asked her questions to keep her awake—about her classes, her hobbies, what kind of music she liked—anything that came to mind.

"My feet are cold," she murmured. "I don't know how I lost my socks." I thought of the warm, new ones I'd put on that morning. It wasn't much, but it was something I could give her. I took them off and carefully pulled them on her feet. I wish I could do something to really help her, I thought. Where is the ambulance?

It seemed like hours went by, as I desperately made conversation to keep Haley conscious. I kept my hand firmly over hers as she shivered, even under all the blankets. At one point, when she complained that her nose itched, I reached out to scratch it for her—just so she wouldn't move.

> *No one is useless in this world who lightens the burden of it for anyone else.*
>
> CHARLES DICKENS

At last sirens sounded in the distance. It had been about twenty-five minutes since my 911 call. "Help's here, Haley," I said, getting to my feet to look for the emergency vehicles.

She tugged on my pant leg. "Don't leave me," she pleaded.

I stayed with her while the paramedics put a body-and-neck brace on her, then strapped her to a gurney. The closest town was too small to handle such a crisis, so the first ambulances were taking only the most critically injured. I stood beside Haley's gurney, holding her hand until an ambulance came for her.

"I'll tell your parents where they're taking you, Haley," I shouted above the sirens as the back doors of the ambulance clanged shut. Slowly, I walked back to my truck.

I talked to her parents later that day, and learned that Haley had suffered a chipped vertebra near her neck, a broken back, and a head wound requiring nine stitches.

While I was with my family, I couldn't stop thinking about Haley. How did the surgery go? Would she be okay? At last I decided I had to know how she was doing. I drove to the hospital in Augusta, Georgia, where she had been admitted.

Love is not an affectionate feeling, but a steady wish for the loved person's ultimate good as far as it can be obtained.

C. S. LEWIS

When I got to Haley's room, her parents rushed over to hug me. "Thank you so much, Gary," her mother told me. "You probably saved Haley's life.

The doctors say that if she had lost consciousness out there on the highway she could have died—or been paralyzed for life if she had tried to get up." I shook my head, stunned. "As it is, she'll be in a body brace for a few months, but after that the doctors think she'll be fine."

Haley smiled at me groggily. I took her hand in mine and squeezed it. "Thank you," she whispered.

When people are serving, life is no longer meaningless.

JOHN W. GARDNER

I didn't do anything, I thought. Yet God had made it possible for me to help Haley simply by being there.

I still worry about my future, but I also have a new faith that God will give me strength to handle whatever lies ahead. We all have more to offer than we know. Whatever I have, I can offer with all my heart. And sometimes that is enough.